From Gangland to Promised Land

Revised Edition 2008

www.xt3media.org

This book is dedicated to the memory of my beloved father Brian Bailey Pridmore who died on 20 September 2004.

I love him and miss him very much. May he rest in peace.

From Gangland to Promised Land

John Pridmore
with Greg Watts

www.xt3media.org

Revised Edition 2008
Published by Xt3 Media
www.xt3media.org

First published in its original form in
2002 by Darton, Longman and Todd Ltd

Reprinted 2002, 2004, 2005, 2006, 2007, 2008.

Cover photography by Saxon Bashford
Cover Design by Dave Moloney

ISBN 0–9547321–3–8
A catalogue record for this book is available
from the British Library.

Published by Xt3 Media (registered charity no 1112003)
Round Foundry Media Centre
Foundry Street
Leeds LS11 5QP
UK
www.xt3media.org
info@xt3media.org

Print Management by
Transform Management Ltd
P.O. Box 2178
Caterham
CR3 6ZT
www.1025transform.co.uk
info@1025transform.co.uk

Contents

Acknowledgements

THERE ARE MANY PEOPLE who have played a part in my life journey; too many to list. So I hope no one will be offended if they are not mentioned. First of all, I would like to thank my family, especially my mum and dad (rest in peace), for the love, patience and understanding they have shown me throughout my life, through the hard times and the good times. I would like to thank my brother David and his children for the blessings they have been in my life, my brothers Bobby and Simon, sisters Emma and Linda, and both sets of grandparents.

I must also acknowledge my stepfather Alan (rest in peace), who gave me my first copy of the New Testament, and my stepmother Elsie. I would also like to thank Bulldog (rest in peace), Douglas Hewitt, David Pracher (rest in peace), Harry Ward, Gary, Neil Slattery, Robert Toone and all my friends at Youth 2000, Mary Anne and Calum Macfarlane-Barrow at the Family House of Prayer, Dalmally, Scotland, Basilia Abel-Smith, Mary, Lesley, Declan, Dominic, Peter and Richard Jones, Stuart Harris, Alex Beverley, Dougie McVicar, and all my Godchildren. I would like to thank Father Brian O'Higgins, whom I first met as a sixteen-year-old when I was in hospital, Father Michael Kelly, who helped me make my first confession and was responsible for me going on my first retreat, Father Pat Deegan, and Father Denis Herlihy, for the wise spiritual direction he has given me. Many other priests have played an important role in my life. I cannot mention them all, but I would especially like to acknowledge Father Richard Aladics, Father Ian Ker, Father William Fraser, Father Conrad, Father Benedict Groeschel, Father Glen Sudano, Father Richard Romer, Father Bernard Murphy, Father Justin Price and Father Fred de l'Orme.

I must also mention Brother Francis. I must also thank Brendan Walsh without whom the original book would not have seen the light of day, Greg Watts for drawing out my memories, thoughts and reflections over many months Land Xt3 Limited my publishers. There is someone else I have to thank, too: Jesus Christ, who is my life and can become yours.

JOHN PRIDMORE

The names of some people and locations have been changed.

One

Son of a policeman

IT WAS THE SUMMER of 1991 and I was working as a doorman, or bouncer, at Nightingales, a popular pub in London's West End. It had been relatively quiet that evening, and I was looking forward to taking a blonde girl who had chatted me up to Stringfellows nightclub. That was one of the perks of working the doors: the endless supply of women.

At the end of the night, as usual, I began walking around the bar, asking people to finish their drinks. Much of the trouble inside pubs and clubs occurs when it's drinking-up time. What many people don't seem to realise is that the doormen don't get paid any extra for hanging around while they take their time finishing their drinks. That's why doormen will hassle people to leave.

I went over to a group of five rowdy blokes in their twenties who were sitting at the top end of the bar. 'Come on, lads. Drink up, please,' I said firmly.

'When I'm ready,' snapped back a very drunk bloke in a white T-shirt.

'Listen,' I replied, leaning across the table, 'you have two minutes and then you're all out. Got it?'

They laughed and carried on sipping their pints.

As I made my way to the far side of the bar to clear the drinkers there, I heard a commotion. Looking round, and seeing two of the other doormen hoisting the drunken blokes towards the door and out into the street, I hurried over to lend a hand.

When I reached the door, the five were shouting and attempting to come back in. Moving swiftly, I blocked their

1

way and, digging my hand into the pocket of my Crombie coat, slipped on my knuckle-duster. While the other doormen were struggling with four of the group, the really drunken one tried to push past me. Oh no you're not, I thought, as I elbowed him back with the full force of my body. He came at me again. This time, I raised my fist and smashed him on the chin, sending him staggering back. Gasping out loud, he collapsed. As his head hit the pavement it exploded, splattering blood everywhere. I quickly slipped the knuckle-duster back into my pocket and waved my hands in the air to show that I had only hit him with my fist. I hadn't expected him to go down like that.

By now, people were panicking and screaming at the sight of the bloke lying there motionless in a pool of blood. The other doormen were standing around, not knowing what to do. Then one of them ran into the office to call an ambulance. Punters began crowding around the bloke on the pavement, looking shocked. I just felt numb, and all this activity became a blur to me.

'He's dead! He's dead!' screamed a girl.

If he was, I thought, it was his own fault. The next moment, I felt a heavy hand on my shoulder. 'Come on, son, you've killed him.'

It was my mate Bulldog, who had come over from east London to have a drink with me.

'Give me your car keys, John. I'll take your car back and you get a cab outside Cairos.'

Bulldog knew that the pub always arranged a cab at Cairos, a club in the next street, if a punter got hurt by a doorman. We did this so that no one saw us leave the pub. I passed him my keys and then quickly made my way through the basement bar and out the back door. When I got to Cairos, Bulldog was already there, sitting in my car. I decided not to take the waiting minicab, but instead to drive back to Leyton myself.

'You've killed the bloke, John. You've got to think what

2

you're going to do,' said Bulldog clinically as we drove along the Strand. Bulldog was a top face in the East End and no stranger to this sort of thing.

'Dunno,' I replied casually, replaying the incident in my mind.

'Is anyone at the pub going to give the Old Bill your full name?'

'No. No one will say anything.'

'Good. Now, do you want some money to go abroad to Spain or somewhere?'

'I've got money, Bulldog,' I answered with a shrug of the shoulders. 'There's no problem. Don't worry. I can handle it.'

My story begins on 4 February 1964 in the Salvation Army Hospital in Hackney, north-east London. As it really was within the sound of Bow Bells, I can call myself a true cockney. My brother David was born in 1961.

We were a working-class family. My mum did odd jobs such as shop work, and my dad was a policeman. Our first home was a three-bedroom semi-detached house in a street called Bridge End in Walthamstow, on the outer edge of London, close to Epping Forest. A busy, built-up area, its greatest claim to fame is that it has the longest street market in Europe. I liked the house, particularly as it had a cellar and a sixty-foot garden at the back.

My mum was born in the Elephant and Castle, in south-east London. She had one sister. My dad was born in Woodford, a short distance from Walthamstow. He was one of six children and, remarkably, his four brothers all became policemen. My parents met when my mum and a friend asked my dad and his beat colleague for directions one evening. They then started going out as a foursome. Mum and Dad got on well, and a couple of years later they were married. At the time, my mum was a practising Catholic. My dad, on the other hand, had been brought up in the Church of England, but had no strong religious beliefs. A condition of Mum agreeing to marry him was that any children be brought up as Catholics.

I think my earliest memory is of the day before my fourth birthday, when my dad asked me whether I wanted to stay at home or go to play school. I told him I wanted to stay at home. For my birthday he gave me a draughts set, with all the pieces shaped like cowboys and Indians.

I cried the whole time on my first day at Thorpe Hall Primary School, which was in Selbourne Road. The head then was a lady called Miss Cobblestick. Even though I was very naughty, she seemed to like me. Every time I was sent to her office, she would give me a sweet from a jar behind her desk. At other times, I used to sit under her desk colouring pictures and being fascinated by the safe which was built into the floor. When Miss Cobblestick left, she was replaced by Mrs Ruttey, who was horrible.

Given the way my life was to develop, it isn't surprising that I was in a gang even at primary school. Near my road was the Liverpool Street-to-Chingford railway line. A footbridge running over it and a subway running under it provided David, my friends and me with a great place to play. Sometimes, however, we couldn't resist playing on the line itself. One day we were caught by the police and given a severe telling-off before they took our names and addresses. I said nothing to my mum and dad when I got home. A week later, my dad returned from work looking very angry. He had found out from one of the officers at the station that I had been playing on the railway line. I was given another telling-off and sent to bed early.

We often used to go to the Granada Cinema in Walthamstow, and because my dad was the home beat officer we would get in for nothing. The cinema manager liked him being there, because if any kids started causing trouble he would eject them. This happened once during *True Grit*, a John Wayne film, when two kids were making a nuisance of themselves. My dad walked over to them, picked them up by their hair and frogmarched them out. I thought the way he did it was brilliant – as good as John Wayne himself.

When I was six, my grandparents on my mum's side drove us to Hastings for the day. (Even though my dad had passed his driving test, he had refused to drive ever since witnessing a horrific road accident one Christmas Day.) With the sun beating down on us, my brother and I paddled in the sea while our grandparents sat on the beach watching us. Mum and Dad had gone off into the town. When they returned, they were holding hands. Smiling, they told us we were going to spend a whole week in Hastings. My brother and I were over the moon and ran across to hug them.

It was a great week, one of those golden memories of childhood that we all have. We stayed above a pub and spent each day in the sea, visiting the castle or on the rides at the funfair. One afternoon, Dad and David went off somewhere by themselves, and Mum and I went for a walk along the sea front, ending up in an Italian restaurant late at night. I can remember she bought me a Horlicks drink in a long glass.

Back at home, on Sundays Dad would often take me to the bar of the Metropolitan Police sports ground, where he would play cards. Once he was playing three-card brag and had a hand of three kings. 'That's a good hand, Dad,' I piped up. 'Three kings!' The other police officers burst into laughter. Dad was not amused.

Dad enjoyed his work as a policeman and always had a fund of stories. I can remember him talking about some of the villains he had met. I once heard him talking about a man who was, he said, the best burglar he had ever come across. His method was to break into a whole row of houses in the early hours of the morning, making his entrance and exit through the back door of each one. He only ever took money. After he had completed his burglaries, he would deposit the money in a large self-addressed brown envelope and drop it into the postbox. That way, if he was ever caught, there would be nothing on him with which the police could charge him.

The sixties were the era of the Kray brothers, the notorious East End gangsters. As a child I was oblivious to this world, but I do recall Dad telling Mum one night, with pride in his voice, that he had pulled up the Krays for speeding and they had been very polite and courteous.

If Mum was working late, Dad would pick us up from school in the police car and take us to the police canteen, where we would wait for him to finish his shift. It was great: all the police officers made a fuss of us and would play snooker with us or give us sweets. I liked the police, mainly, I think, because they had a certain power and authority.

Like any child, I always felt there was a real magic about Christmas. The week before Christmas, my dad would take me on the tube to the West End to choose my Christmas presents. Looking at all the toys in Hamley's and Selfridges was fantastic. Afterwards we would walk to Piccadilly Circus and have a meal in a restaurant and then go to the cinema. I would often fall asleep on the tube on the way back home.

Religion played little part in my childhood. My mum drifted away from her Catholic faith soon after I was born, and would only go to church sporadically. She used to take me to Mass when I was about three, but I found it boring. Later on, going to the dog track or stock-car racing with my dad always seemed more interesting than sitting in a dreary church. Yet each time Mum and I walked past the church where I had been baptised, she would always remind me of it. I was, however, always fascinated by God, even at that age, and I once asked an aunt to buy me a children's Bible.

I have a lot of happy memories from those early years of my childhood. My happiest memory, I think, comes from just before my tenth birthday. I had always wanted a pet dog. One day my dad pulled up outside in the police car with his driver. He came in with a shoebox, put it on the table and said, 'This is for you.' When I took the lid off, I leapt for joy. Inside was a tiny Labrador puppy. I couldn't contain my excitement, and ran to my dad and hugged him. 'I hope he's worth it,' he laughed. 'He's just been sick all over the police car!' Looking back at those first ten years, I felt secure, content, loved and valued.

The night when I received the news that was to shatter my childhood occurred when I was eleven. I came running into the kitchen after Sea Scouts, only to find my mum and dad rowing. I had never seen Dad look so angry. When they saw me, they ordered me upstairs. I found my brother sobbing in their bed. He refused to tell me what Mum and Dad were arguing about, but mentioned a word I hadn't heard before: divorce.

A bit later, Mum and Dad came upstairs and sat on either side of the bed. 'Boys, you are going to have to choose who you want to live with,' said Dad slowly and deliberately.

'Why, Dad?' I asked, unable to understand the question. 'Is this a game?'

'We're getting divorced,' replied my mum with tears in her eyes.

I still didn't know what they meant. 'Why do I have to choose who I want to live with? I live with you both. You're my mum and dad.'

David remained silent and looked tearful. He seemed to understand what they were talking about. That night in our bedroom, he tried to explain that Mum and Dad were going to live in different places, so we had to decide which of them we wanted to live with.

'But why?' I protested. 'Why are they going to live in separate places? It doesn't make sense.' I was deeply confused. Looking back, I think I made an unconscious decision not to love any more, because then I couldn't be hurt.

Over the next few weeks, Mum became very withdrawn and said very little to us. Then one day Dad told us she was going away for a while – to Claybury. I was shocked at this. At school Claybury was known as 'the nutters' home', and sometimes kids would be told, 'You should be in Claybury.' Claybury was, in fact, a psychiatric hospital.

The house seemed empty and cold after Mum walked out with her suitcase one day and got into a car with a stranger. Each night, when I came back from school, I still expected to find her there. I would often cry myself to sleep, wondering why she had gone and when I would see her again.

After a while, David and I were allowed to visit her after school. We would catch a bus from Walthamstow to just outside Chigwell and then walk along a main road before taking the lane that led to Claybury. The hospital was a huge, gloomy Victorian building set in sprawling grounds. Every time I walked down its long corridors I could smell disinfectant. Often I wanted to vomit.

Mum seemed different at Claybury. David told me she was taking tablets to make her better. Some of the other patients in the hospital used to frighten me. They would wander around muttering to themselves, or sit in the lounge staring into space and chain-smoking. At times, I would hear shouting and screaming coming from somewhere in the hospital. It was an awful place.

I began to find myself feeling angry towards Dad, because I felt he was responsible for Mum leaving. I also felt angry towards Mum, because I thought she should be at home with us. By now I was attending Chapel End Secondary School, and the anger inside me was spilling out into the classroom. I got into fights, messed around in class and was generally disruptive in any way I could find. I would regularly fight boys older than me, and developed a reputation as a bit of a head case. The school knew I had to visit Mum, so they never gave me detentions – but I probably got caned more than any other pupil there.

At home I started to be cheeky to Dad, and refused to do what he told me. I knew this was hurting him. I would say I was going to live with Mum when she came out of Claybury. I missed her terribly. To let Dad know how I felt, one day I deliberately smashed a target game he had bought me. It was one of my favourite toys, but I desperately wanted to show him how I felt.

Mum became confused during her stay at Claybury. Sometimes when I visited her she would ask me to leave, sometimes she would hug me. I was worried about her, as she seemed to be becoming like some of the other patients. I had accepted that she wasn't well, and wondered if she would ever come out of Claybury. It only added to my sense of insecurity when, shortly after Mum had gone into Claybury, Dad announced that we were leaving our home and moving to a two-bedroom police flat in The Drive in Walthamstow.

As I look back now on that very traumatic period of my life, one thing stands out: no one asked me how I felt; no one asked how the break-up was affecting me. Although my grandparents across the river at Walworth Road made a big fuss of me when I went there at weekends, even they never asked me what was going on inside my head. This made me even more angry. I felt very alone at that time. It was probably because I felt so isolated and ignored that I began stealing money from my dad.

It had looked as if Mum was going to be in Claybury for some years, but after one year she came out and moved into Forest House, a rehabilitation hostel connected to the hospital. Years later, she told me that the treatment had helped her, and also that my granddad had had a Mass said for her. She got a job in the office of a furniture company near my school. Just a few years before, she had been working as a secretary at a wine merchants in the City.

I remember Dad being worried about a rash I had developed and taking me to the doctor. The doctor suggested that it was due to stress, and recommended that I didn't see Mum, as he thought this was causing the problem. It was hard for Dad, looking after David and me and working as a policeman. He had to make a lot of sacrifices, and I know now that he placed our needs above his own.

Mum began visiting me in my school lunch hour. She would

wait for me in the playground and then take me for something to eat in a nearby café. I began to treasure these meetings. One day, Dad turned up at the school and found Mum there. He told her that the doctor had said it was better if she didn't see me for a while. Watching them argue about this, I felt helpless and in pain. The fact that my mum was coming to the school to see me had made me feel special, for once.

After that, I didn't see Mum for about six months, which is an incredibly long time for a child to be without a parent. One day I was walking down a street near the school when my heart leapt: Mum was walking towards me. She didn't notice me, though, and walked right past me. I called after her and she turned round. A smile lit up her face, and she gave me a big hug. That night, I told my dad I'd met Mum, and that my rash had gone. He agreed that I could see her again.

The pain I felt during those six months was eased a little by a friendship I made with another boy of my age, Simon. I first met him when he pushed in front of me in the dinner queue at school and I beat him up. We later became friends when we discovered we both liked snakes and playing at being soldiers. I was amazed that his uncle kept snakes in a glass case in the living room. Simon and I were given permission to go on a weekend camping holiday to Southend-on-Sea. Clive, Simon's mum's boyfriend, had agreed to give us a lift and bring us back, and my dad took me round to Simon's house. Soon Simon's mum Elsie and my dad started spending a lot of time with each other, and Clive disappeared off the scene.

Simon and I thought it would be great if my dad and his mum were to get married, because that would mean we would be together as brothers. Simon also had two sisters, Emma, aged six, and Linda, aged eighteen. A couple of weeks later we all moved into a police flat in Romford. It wasn't long, however, before Dad and Elsie were arguing. For two families to live under one roof isn't easy, and Dad and Elsie had different views about how to raise a family.

By this time, Mum was working in the Co-op and living in a one-bedroom flat in Leyton. She and Dad were now divorced, and she was going out with a man called Alan. David and I would often spend a weekend with her. Alan liked me and sometimes he would take me for a ride on his motorbike.

One Saturday I let myself into the flat, as I often did because Mum had given me a key, and I found a suitcase in the bedroom. Curious, I opened it and discovered it was stuffed with five and ten pound notes. The temptation was too great, and I helped myself to a wad and stuffed the money into my trouser pocket. Each time I went to the flat after that, I took more money. Simon and I would spend it on takeaways, restaurant meals (where we were allowed to drink beer), and days out in Southend. Once in Southend I paid for about fifty laps on the go-kart track!

I had now moved to Reading Court School in Harold Hill. I did quite well in exams because I had a good memory, but I found it difficult to pay attention in class. I would mess about, even if the lesson was being taught by the strictest teacher. Apart from art, I had little interest in the subjects we studied. I couldn't see the point. I just didn't want to be in school for seven hours a day, and I didn't try to disguise the fact. Compared to Chapel End, Reading Court was very lax. I only ever got caned once.

I was also now shoplifting. The first time I did it was when Dad gave me some money to buy a pair of trainers. I went into a shoe shop, stuffed the trainers under my jacket and walked out. It seemed so easy, and I began nicking regularly. I didn't do it for the money. Most of the things I stole were useless. I just did it for the excitement.

One afternoon, I was caught by a store detective in Littlewoods in Romford. When the police arrived, they searched me and discovered I had some napkin holders in my pocket. I admitted I had nicked them from Debenhams, and was put in the back of a police car and taken to Romford police station. When Dad turned up, he told me he wasn't surprised by what I had done because of my general behaviour.

The following week, I had to return to the police station with Dad to be cautioned. He didn't seem worried about this and was cracking jokes on the bus journey there. What's more, he seemed more concerned about me than other police officers might think. After an inspector gave me a caution, he told me sternly that if I continued to shoplift I could be sent away to borstal.

This incident, and the threat of borstal, did little to dampen my enthusiasm for thieving. The reason why I was stealing was to get some attention. I had felt ignored after Mum and Dad split up. Apart from Simon and David, no one seemed interested in my feelings.

One day, Mum's boyfriend Alan rang my dad to tell him that I had been stealing money. Over a few months I had, it turned out, nicked £1,400.

'What's been going on, John?' asked Dad.

'It's because you and Mum divorced,' I replied.

'What do you mean?'

'I wanted to get back at you both.'

That night, my dad spoke to me about what he feared might happen. 'As a policeman, I've seen lots of kids go down this road, and it leads to disaster. I care about you, John, and I don't want you to end up the same way.'

When I next met Alan, I feared the worst. Instead, he sat me down and said he forgave me. He spoke to me with a lot of love, but he wanted to know why I had taken the money. I muttered that it was simply greed. I didn't feel able to say that, while there was an element of truth in this, the main reason was the hurt I felt over the divorce. I didn't blame Alan for the divorce. That was Mum's and Dad's doing. Realising that I had disappointed and hurt Alan – who was, I knew, a good and kind bloke – I felt very guilty.

It didn't stop me, though. I swiftly graduated from shop-lifting to breaking and entering with two kids my age, Chris and Kenny. Chris was quite fat and always wore a Liverpool football shirt, while Kenny was thin, spotty and looked as if he needed a good wash. I used to climb out of my bedroom window, jump down onto a ledge and then jump to the ground. I would meet Chris and Kenny on the main road, usually at about 3 a.m. We would break into schools, park huts, factories – all sorts of places. Once we nicked a load of golf putters and balls, and had great fun with them in the park the next day.

We did it for the excitement, not really because we wanted the things we stole. It was a bonus if we came across any money, as we did once when we broke into my school. I think my dad knew I was creeping out at night, because he used to place matchsticks against the front and back doors to see if they had been moved.

It was only a matter of time before I was caught. It happened one night when Chris and I broke into a pet shop. For some reason I can't remember, we planned to nick some white mice. Someone must have seen us clambering over the wall at the back of the shop, however, for within five minutes the police had arrived and we were caught red-handed and taken to Romford police station. During the interview we also both admitted to breaking into a car that night. We were charged and then driven home.

My dad hit the roof when he found out what had happened. A few weeks later, I appeared in court and was found guilty of aggravated burglary, because Chris had been carrying a flick knife. My punishment was twenty-four hours at an attendance centre in Harold Hill. This meant that for two hours every Saturday afternoon for twelve weeks I had to do PE and carpentry. I hated it, but it didn't deter me from continuing to break into places.

A few weeks later, during the summer holidays, we broke into our school again, tempted by the prospect of dinner

13

money. This time, however, the office was locked. We kicked and pushed the door, but we couldn't open it. Furious, we then began smashing up everything in sight. By the time our rage had subsided, we had caused thousands of pounds worth of damage and left parts of the school looking as if they had been hit by a bomb.

Two days later, I looked out of the front window and froze. Two policemen were walking towards the door. They told a shocked Elsie that they had a search warrant. Elsie demanded to know what had happened, but I just shrugged my shoulders and sat there in the living room waiting for the inevitable. There was no point in running. I had to face the music.

After a few minutes, the policemen walked into the living room carrying various nicked items they had found under my bed. I was arrested, put in the police car and taken to Romford police station to be charged. The police had also found stolen stuff in Chris' and Kenny's homes, and they too had been charged. The three of us were scheduled to appear at Romford Magistrates' Court a fortnight later.

That night at home, my dad had a very worried look on his face when he told me he wanted to have a serious talk with me. 'John, this time I don't think you're going to be so lucky. You're probably going to be sent away. My advice is to make a clean break and own up to whatever else you have done. If you don't, you're going to find yourself in more trouble at some point. Do it as TICs [Taken into Considerations], John.'

I listened to Dad, who spoke more out of concern for me than out of anger over what I had done, and decided he was right. It was going to be bad enough if I was sent away. If that happened, then I didn't want charges coming back at me. My aim would be to get out as quickly as possible and stay out.

In court, my dad acted as my solicitor and I admitted to about sixty offences of theft. What I didn't know before the court hearing was that Chris and Kenny had broken into a farm and stolen a shotgun. Even though it didn't have any cartridges, it placed us all in a bad light. When the magistrate recommended that the three of us be sent to borstal, a cold sweat came over me. I had heard all about borstal. It was meant to be brutal. Suddenly, faced with the prospect of this, what I had become came home to me. The magistrate added that the final decision could only be taken by a judge at the crown court. He ruled that, in the meantime, the three of us should be put on licence to our parents.

When I walked into Chelmsford Crown Court on the September morning of my case, I was met by a barrister my dad had appointed through a solicitor called Sherwin. A few years later, I was to meet Sherwin himself and when I did, I learned how money could buy a not-guilty verdict.

'If you get court one,' said the barrister matter-of-factly, 'you will be up before Judge Greenwood and there will be nothing I can do: you will get sent to borstal.'

Then I heard my name called over the tannoy, followed by the words 'court one'. That was it, I thought, as I stood up. I was done for now. But then I was told that Judge Greenwood had been moved to another court and a different judge would be sitting. My spirits rose at this, and I smiled nervously at my dad.

After the judge had heard from Chris' barrister, he asked if Kenny's and mine were going to say the same thing. When they said yes, they were, he ordered a ten-minute recess. I sat in court, feeling that my life was slipping away from me. What was the judge going to order? Might he decide to send me to an attendance centre instead? That wouldn't be too bad, compared to borstal. Or he might even let me off.

Eventually he came back out, sat down, cleared his throat and addressed the court. 'Now, given the ages of the three defendants, I am going to be very lenient. They are, I am told, aware of the serious nature of their offences. I hope that they may have learned a lesson from all this. So, I sentence the three defendants to three months in a detention centre.'

I put my head in my hands. I hadn't got borstal, but a

detention centre still meant being banged up. Chris and Kenny looked as shocked as I did. Were we really going to be sent away for three months?

Dad came over to me, placed his hand gently on my shoulder and said with emotion in his voice, 'Sorry, John.'

Two

Sent down

DURING THE LONG JOURNEY TO Kidlington Detention Centre in Oxfordshire I sank into a deep depression, listening to Kenny's horror stories of what it would be like there. Sitting in the van, I reflected that my freedom had now been taken away from me. When I got up, what I ate, where I went, what I did, when I went to bed: someone else was now going to decide all this. I was just fifteen, and I was missing Mum, Dad, David and Simon.

My first view of Kidlington only increased my anxiety. Set back from the road, it was a large, drab building, a bit like a school, and its walls were topped with barbed wire. The message was clear: if you think you're coming here for a holiday, forget it. The centre seemed to be miles from anywhere.

The three of us were booked in, searched, briskly told the rules by a tough-looking member of staff, given a purple jacket and trousers, blue T-shirt, underwear, shoes, socks and a number, and were then led to our dormitories, which were spartan and cold. Each of us was allocated a bed and a bedside cabinet for our possessions. We discovered that there were another seventy or so youths there, most in for three months like us. The next morning the three of us were ordered to see the barber, who gave each of us the standard short back and sides. This was another way of taking away our individuality. I hated losing my long hair.

The Kidlington regime was governed by the bell. We had little free time, and when we did have some, there wasn't much to do with it. There was no TV, radio, snooker or table

17

tennis. The idea was that you were deprived of all treats. An average day at Kidlington started at 6 a.m. After a shower, we all had to go on parade outside before having breakfast. Next came morning jobs, then lunch at 1 p.m., followed by classes in English, maths and other subjects. After the evening meal, we all had to sit in silence with a library book before trooping off for another class. Lights out was at 10 p.m.

During our first week, Chris and I were walking to the dining room when a large Asian youth slapped Chris on the back really hard. I discovered later that this youth was in for six months because he had assaulted a policeman. He was clearly looking for a fight, but Chris told him to get lost and then ignored him. Later, Chris, Kenny and I decided to teach the Asian youth a lesson. We all knew that in a place such as Kidlington you had to stand up for yourself. What's more, Chris wanted revenge. So we got hold of the buffers that were used for polishing the floor, and hid them in our beds. That night, after lights out, we crept across the dormitory to the Asian youth's bed. He was fast asleep. The three of us laid into him with the buffers, and he woke up screaming. We carried on whacking him and then hurried back to our beds before one of the staff heard his screams. Two of the staff arrived, demanding to know what was happening, but the three of us just pretended to be asleep. The following morning we were questioned about the incident, but we brazenly denied knowing anything about it.

The subject that I and most of the lads hated the most was PE, which often consisted of a long run. The instructors were army types who always seemed to be shouting. In order to get out of the Wednesday afternoon PE class, I used to go with a few other lads to see the Catholic priest for an hour. He would give us tea and biscuits and chat to us about our lives. I remember looking forward to these sessions – but I think it had more to do with the tea and biscuits than with any interest in religion!

Some of the screws were vicious. Penal institutions often

attract two kinds of people: those who see their role in terms of caring, and those who are on a power trip. One small lad who used to wet his bed was made fun of by both the screws and the other lads. I felt sorry for him. It became so bad that he tried to escape one day, but he was caught. One of my jobs that day was to take a cup of tea to the doctor, who visited the centre most weeks. When I reached the door of the medical room, I could hear screaming inside. Opening it, I was shocked to see the doctor laying into the kid with his fists.

When I look back on my time at Kidlington, I can see that many of the lads there were very damaged. The strict, uncaring regime only made matters worse, although I got used to it and even began to enjoy it. I even read my first book while I was there, a Western. There wasn't really much trouble from other lads, because they were frightened of being caught by the screws. As long as you didn't try to buck the system, the screws, generally, didn't hassle you.

In places like Kidlington, or in any prison, you learn different strokes from the other inmates. I got on well with Terry, a wiry kid who looked as if butter wouldn't melt in his mouth. When he told me about all the stuff he had got up to, he reminded me of the Artful Dodger in the film *Oliver!* – breaking and entering, pickpocketing, robbery, shoplifting, fraud, he'd done the lot.

A screw said to me that the first day my mum came to visit I would be crying like everyone else. No way, I replied confidently, and I never did cry. I wasn't going to show that I was weak, like some of the lads. Visiting was only allowed on Saturday afternoons, when a snack bar selling sweets and biscuits would be open. While I was there I was visited by Dad, Mum, Alan, Granddad and Nan.

Finally, one day in December 1979, the morning of my release arrived. Underneath a grey sky, I boarded a special coach to London, clutching a plastic bag containing my few possessions, relieved to be returning home. My mum was

19

waiting for me at the set-down point in Victoria. When I saw her smiling face, I felt free – and loved – once again. Inhaling the city air felt good, I thought, as Mum and I made our way through the crowds to the tube station. When we got to her flat, she cooked me a great big meal, which I gobbled down, having spent the last three months eating boring and horrible food.

Later that night I went home to my dad's place, happy to be returning to familiarity. My heart sank, however, when I discovered that life with Dad and Elsie was worse than before. Their arguments were now happening on a daily basis, and there was always tension in the flat. They can't carry on like this for much longer, I thought, remembering the arguments that had led to Dad splitting with Mum.

I was right. A few weeks later, Dad decided to leave Elsie. He, David and I went to live in a flat in Harold Hill. Things worked out well between the three of us, although I missed not having Simon around. A few weeks later, however, Dad moved back in with Elsie and left David and me on our own. David, who was now eighteen and working, shared the cost of the rent with Dad.

I was due to leave school at Easter, but had no idea what I would do. I couldn't think of any career that excited me. I had no interest in any of the subjects we studied at school, and just stared into space when one of the teachers tried to talk to me about my future. What did they know? I continued to get into trouble, which is what some of the teachers expected anyway, I think. Like a number of others, I couldn't wait to leave and start earning some real money – one way or the other.

The owner of the electrical shop where I had worked as a Saturday boy offered me a full-time job, and I took it. At the beginning this seemed fine, but before long I was getting restless and feeling that fifty quid was not much for five days' work. I began dipping my hand in the till when the owner was out of the shop.

The memories of Kidlington had faded fast. At the back of my mind, I knew that if I was caught I might end up somewhere much worse than Kidlington next time, now that I was sixteen and eligible to be sent to a youth prison. Yet each time you steal and get away with it, the temptation to do it again is too strong to resist.

One afternoon, I was riding my motorbike through Harold Wood when I suddenly lost control. The next thing I remember was that I was lying in a hospital ward, racked with pain. I had broken my leg in twenty-eight places and bone had come through the skin, and I had also dislocated my shoulder. I was in hospital for several months. One day a Catholic priest appeared on the ward and introduced himself as Father Brian O'Higgins. He was the hospital chaplain, and he had noticed from the admission register that I had put down 'RC' as my religion. A warm man, he sat by my bedside and chatted with me. After that, he used to pop in to see me regularly.

On the day of my discharge from hospital, Father Brian gave me a lift home. Over the next few months, I had several meals with him at the presbytery and got involved in his parish youth club in Harold Hill. He also occasionally took me to the opera and art galleries. He never spoke about Jesus, but he showed me a lot of love. I remember that one day he gave me a sketchbook which had a picture of St Thomas More in it. I don't know why, but I felt a real closeness to this rather serious-looking man who, Father Brian told me, had been imprisoned in the Tower of London and executed for his faith.

Since the owner of the electrical shop had refused to pay me while I was in hospital, I returned to work early. As a result, I contracted septicaemia and had to have another stay in hospital. When I went back to the shop after that, I felt quite angry with the owner and began nicking larger amounts of money. One day, when he sent me out to get a set of keys cut, I got a second set done for myself, so that I could come

21

and go when I liked. I began nicking blank video tapes from the shop and selling them elsewhere.

Although I'd had a couple of girlfriends at school, I had my first serious relationship around this time, with Louise, a beautiful mixed-race girl. On our first date, I took her to a posh West End restaurant, where there were roses on the table and romantic music playing in the background. Afterwards we went to see *Evita*, starring Elaine Paige and David Cassidy. During the interval we drank Harvey Wallbangers. 'I think they've gone to my head!' she laughed, putting her arms around me. Then I kissed her for the first time. Sitting on the tube on the way home, we kissed and cuddled, oblivious to the other people in the carriage, and I felt really proud to be with such a beautiful woman. Over the next few months we saw a lot of each other, and I used to stay overnight at her flat when her father was on night shifts. I think we really loved each other, but I found it difficult to maintain the relationship. I was lacking in confidence, and I didn't feel good enough for her.

One night, as I was coming out of the shop with a bag of blank videos, a police car pulled up and I was nicked. At Walthamstow I was charged with theft from an employer, and also with breaking into a Metropolitan Police sports centre.

Two weeks later I was standing in court listening to the magistrate give me a three-month sentence to a young offenders' institution. I was put in the back of a prison van and taken to Hollesley Bay, near Ipswich in Suffolk.

Upon arrival, I was bundled out of the police van, given a brisk medical by the doctor and taken to the hospital, which was a separate building from the prison, as my leg was still ulcerated as a result of the motorbike accident. The cells were small and only contained a wash basin and a bed. Once a week you could choose a book from the library trolley, but there were never more than a couple of dozen books to choose from. The days at Hollesley Bay were incredibly long and the regime was worse than at Kidlington. Unless you

22

have been locked up in a cell for twenty-three hours a day, as I was, you can't really understand how long days can seem – just hours stretching out in front of you with nothing to look forward to, no TV, no treats, nothing. Through my cell window I could see the beach and the sea beyond the barbed-wire fence. This only heightened the sense of having lost my freedom.

I learned that some of those in the hospital were on a 'Section 43'. This meant that they were there for their own protection, not because of any medical problem. I soon realised that one way of getting out of the cell was to do tasks around the prison, so one day I volunteered myself to one of the screws. A few days later I had a job filing papers in one of the offices. It was mindless work, but better than being cooped up in the cell.

Things got so bad at one point that I found myself contemplating suicide as I lay on my bed, staring at the ceiling. That would be one way of putting an end to the misery and boredom, I figured. Thankfully, I never quite reached that level of desperation. At the time, I thought it was anger that kept me alive. Only later was I to realise what really saved me.

Like many of the other blokes there, I spent a lot of time sleeping. When I wasn't sleeping, I was forced to think. This was uncomfortable. I remember writing two letters, one to my mum and one to my dad. I told them I felt my life was a failure, and said how sorry I was for hurting them through the things I had done. I felt I had really hit rock bottom. What would be waiting for me when I was released from prison? Nothing. I had no job, no money and nowhere to stay. My life was empty and the future dark.

Three

Back in court

STARING OUT OF THE WINDOW as the train rolled through the Suffolk countryside, I thought how good it was to see green fields and trees again. You really miss that in prison. I looked at the reflection of my face, and told myself that I was never going to end up back inside.

'So what you gonna do, then, when you get back to Walthamstow, John?' asked one of the blokes who had been released with me.

'See my mates, make a lot of dough,' I grinned. 'What about you?'

His face lit up. 'The first thing I want to do is hug my kids.'

I wasn't going to stay with either of my parents, I reflected, as the familiar rooftops and tower blocks of east London came into view. I felt anger towards them, although it was buried deep inside me. Their divorce had caused me a great deal of hurt. Sue, the probation officer, would find me somewhere, I consoled myself.

My brother David, who worked in the stationery department at Merrill Lynch in the City, had asked to meet me in a pub next to Liverpool Street station. He said he'd take an early lunch hour. He waved to me from the bar as soon as I walked through the door, and then came straight over and hugged me. I felt a bit awkward, as he'd never done that before. I appreciated him welcoming me home, though, and realised probably for the first time the deep love he had for me.

'So, what was it like in there, John?' he asked with a serious expression.

I shrugged my shoulders. 'Nah, you know, not too bad. Could have been worse.' I wasn't going to let him know that I had contemplated suicide. I was unable to share something so intimate, even with my brother. If I did, I might get hurt.

I made my way to Sue's office in Walthamstow. She gave me the address of a bed and breakfast a few miles away in Chingford. As I stood up to leave, I tapped her for some money and she took twenty pounds out of a biscuit tin in a filing cabinet. Holding it out, she warned me not to spend it on drink and gambling. 'Of course not,' I replied.

After a few pints and games of pool in The Bell, I caught the bus to Chingford and walked to the bed and breakfast hotel, which was opposite the police station. The landlady, a small, middle-aged Italian woman, told me the room was seven quid a night with breakfast and that I needed to provide a ten quid deposit for the room and a two quid deposit for the key. She gave me a letter confirming the rates.

The following morning, I caught the bus back to Walthamstow and went to the social security office. Like all DHSS offices, it was scruffy and dreary and the air smelt stale. Graffiti had been scrawled on the peeling grey walls, and cigarette butts lay scattered on the floor. Before joining the queue, I took out the crumpled letter from the Italian lady and altered the £10 to £100 and the £2 to £20. There's no way they'll know I've done it, I told myself. I swaggered up to the counter, where I was confronted by a stern, plump woman with thick glasses. What a miserable old cow, I thought to myself. I shoved the letter from the Italian lady and a letter from the prison under the partition and tapped my fingers as she examined them. 'Is this correct?' she said in a school-mistressy voice.

I glared at her. 'It's the bed and breakfast receipt, innit?'

She shot me a disbelieving look and told me to come back at 3 p.m.

I returned to the DHSS office just before three and took a seat, expecting another long wait, but my name was called after just a few minutes. Oh no, I thought as I approached the small office and peered ahead through the window in the door, it's that miserable old cow again.

'Sit down, Mr Pridmore,' she commanded as I walked in. Then she added sarcastically, 'I've got someone to see you. I'm sure you'll be pleased to see them.'

Instinctively, I turned round. My heart sank. There were two stony-faced rozzers standing behind me. The woman had such a sneering look on her face that I just wanted to give her a slap, even though I would never actually hit a woman. She knew I'd just got out of prison, and yet it made no difference to her. She had, it turned out, phoned the Italian lady to verify the letter. There was nothing for it but to come clean.

I was taken to Chingford police station and charged on two counts of fraud. After several hours they released me, and I returned to the bed and breakfast. The landlady was angry that I had lied to the DHSS, and she refused to return my suitcase until I paid her the money I owed. That night, I slept on the grass across the road.

The next day, I met a mate of mine called Stuart, who said I could sleep on the floor of his bedsit until I got sorted out. Stuart was very thin, had long hair and was a very timid, smooth character who wore brightly coloured Pringle jumpers. His parents were divorced, like mine, and that seemed to give us a common bond.

'Listen, John,' said Stuart. 'Bomber's planning to do the clothes shop along the road. Do you fancy it?'

I knew the clothes shop. They had some nice gear in it; the kind you could easily sell in the pubs and on the estates. Even though it would be risky, I agreed. I was desperate for some cash, and I needed to get my suitcase back.

The following night, Stuart's mates Bomber and Smiley came to the bedsit. They both had skinhead-type haircuts and tattoos. Smiley was a short guy, with a British Movement tattoo on the inside of his lip and an 'M' on one of his cheeks.

26

Bomber was about six foot four and had got his nickname because he had a temper and would explode like a bomb. Like me, they'd done quite a bit of nicking, but unlike me, they'd never been caught. They were both into body-building and fighting. I'd been with them a few times to the gym in Walthamstow High Street, which was run by a guy who had been Mr Universe and had, appropriately, married a Miss World.

At about 3 a.m. we left the flat and made our way into the deserted street. 'Right,' whispered Bomber, his eyes darting to and fro. 'Let's do it. And remember, it's straight in, grab the gear, and then straight out again.' We knew the layout of the shop, so we knew exactly what to go for.

Stuart and Smiley nodded and we hurried along the street, looking around anxiously in case anyone rumbled us. Smiley kept watch on the street as Bomber and I flung the lead at the two windows. There was an almighty crash, followed by the sound of an alarm going off. Then Bomber, Stuart and I dived in, booting the glass out of the way and making sure that we weren't cut to pieces. My heart was pounding as I quickly gathered up some jeans and leather jackets, knocking over a rack in the process. Stuart had a pile of men's jackets in his arms and Bomber had gone for some long coats.

The alarm was still ringing loudly as we legged it with the gear down the street, around the corner into the alley and in through the back door of Stuart's building. Breathless and tense, we raced up the stairs and back into the bedsit. We hid some of the gear behind the fireplace, and Bomber and Smiley took the rest with them.

At about 8 a.m., I was woken up by a loud banging at the door.

'Police! Open up.'

I froze. Stuart sat bolt upright and then scrambled out of bed and climbed into his trousers. Two rozzers marched in when he opened the door. 'Sorry to disturb you, lads,' said the one with the moustache, 'but the clothes shop a few doors along has been broken into. Mind if we have a look around? We found some coat hangers in the alley round the back.'

We watched anxiously as they searched the room. 'No, nothing here,' concluded the smaller one disappointedly, straightening up after looking under the bed. As they closed the door behind them, Stuart and I grinned at each other and immediately began talking about how we were going to sell the gear. As it was good stuff, it would be dead easy.

Later that day, I went to see Bill Sherwin, my solicitor. I told him exactly what had happened at the DHSS, and asked him what he thought my defence should be. He was as bent as a nine bob note and claimed he could get you off any charge, if you paid enough money. He could even nobble a jury if you had twenty-five grand.

I waited anxiously to see what plan of action he would come up with. He sat back in his swivel chair and joined his hands, twiddling a thick gold ring around his finger. As usual, he was wearing a pinstripe suit with a pink shirt and flashy tie. 'I'll get you on the right day,' he said confidently. He could tell by my puzzled look that I didn't have a clue what he meant.

When I met Sherwin on the morning of my case a couple of weeks later, he told me to sit at the back of court number one. Strange, I thought, noticing that it was all blokes sitting there. What was Sherwin up to?

Anyway, the first two went into the dock and the clerk read out the charge: gross indecency. The three magistrates sat expressionless. The men had been caught hanging around Whipps Cross Hospital toilets, a well-known haunt of homosexuals. Then two more were called and the clerk read out the charges: again gross indecency. By this time the chief magistrate, a crusty old army major type with one of those leathered faces, was getting more and more wound up. Then another bloke was called. Once again, the clerk read out charges of gross indecency. I looked across at Sherwin, wondering what was going on. His expression gave nothing away.

The magistrate had started off with a fifty quid fine, but as the procession of shamefaced men appeared before him the fines went up and up – a hundred quid, two hundred, three hundred. The last blokes were given something like a six hundred quid fine. When I was eventually called, the magistrate's face was ready to explode. I could see what he was thinking. I was for it.

All three magistrates eyed me distastefully as I entered the dock, trying to look as repentant as I could, while the clerk looked down at his sheet of paper.

'The defendant is charged with two counts of defrauding the Department of Health and Social Security, your honour.'

'Well, I have to say, it's nice to get back to good, honest villainy,' interrupted the crusty magistrate, his face relaxing. The two magistrates sitting on either side of him chuckled.

A policeman then described what had happened at the DHSS. Next, Sherwin stood up and explained that I had committed the crime because I had no money. 'Your honour,' he continued, passing a blue folder to the clerk, 'my client's probation officer has explained that the situation arose out of his compulsive gambling.'

The clerk handed the folder to the crusty magistrate. He studied it for a few moments and then addressed Sherwin. 'In view of the facts you have presented, Mr Sherwin, I have decided to treat your client leniently.'

Turning to me, he said solemnly, 'Mr Pridmore, on this occasion I will fine you fifty pounds on each of the charges. And I won't order you to be returned to prison.'

Blimey, I thought, sneaking a glance at Sherwin, who had a big smirk on his face. 'Er, thank you, your honour,' I stuttered.

'The defendant will have no costs to pay,' said the magistrate, adding after a pause, 'I think the DHSS can afford them.'

Afterwards, sitting in The Bell across the road, Sherwin looked very pleased with himself. He said he'd arranged for me to appear after the men charged with gross indecency because he knew the magistrate couldn't stand homosexuals.

I felt a huge sense of relief. I had been so close to going back down. What now? I felt I needed my own place, and with the money from the gear we'd flogged I could get somewhere. Stuart's bedsit had been okay for a while, but it was cramped and I think we were beginning to get on each other's nerves.

I desperately needed some regular money, so I answered an advert for a carver at a plush hotel in Victoria. To my surprise, I was taken on immediately. The head chef really seemed to like me and the wages were very good, considering that my cooking skills were limited to preparing beans on toast. It turned out, when I reported for work on the first day, that the chef had somehow mistaken me for a sous chef. I thought I had better come clean with him. When the chef de partie heard how I had got one past the head chef, he thought it was hilarious and found me another job in the kitchen.

It wasn't long before I had my own place to stay. I rented the bottom room in a house owned by a Nigerian man and his family. The family soon went off to Nigeria and left me alone in the house, although they locked all their rooms. One day a letter came for the owner. I could tell the envelope contained a cashpoint card. I opened it, and there was a form to be signed and returned. I'd found a signed cheque on the table in the hallway one day, so I thought I'd have a go at forging the man's signature. I sent off the form, and a week later the PIN number arrived.

For the first time since being released from prison, I had some serious money to play with. I drew about two hundred pounds per day from cashpoints and blew it all in pubs, with the bookies, and on some decent gear to wear. I was into caps, tweed jackets and leather gloves at that time: I wanted to be different.

A few weeks later, I was called into the personnel office at the hotel. Two CID officers were waiting for me. I felt the ground open up beneath me, and I knew instantly that my scam with the cashpoint card had been discovered. They put me into a car and took me across London to Leyton police station.

When questioned, I told the police that there were other people living in the house and I knew nothing about the cashpoint card. Eventually they bailed me, as they didn't have enough evidence to charge me. Nevertheless, the hotel sacked me. Having the police turn up was clearly not good for business.

With my Nigerian landlord due back any day, I thought it was time to hop it. I figured he wouldn't look too kindly on me if he found out that I had milked his bank account of over two thousand pounds. I found a bedsit for a short time and then, when I didn't have the money for the rent, moved to a dingy bed and breakfast above an off-licence in Leytonstone High Road. I shared a room with three other blokes, all unemployed but doing a bit of work on the side.

A mate told me about a shop on Commercial Road where you could get hold of dodgy perfume and socks and stuff. I began flogging these goods in Oxford Street and outside Stratford underground station. As usual, however, I spent the money as soon as I got it.

Gary is really the only person I've kept in touch with from those days. We first met when the landlord sold his off-licence and moved us all to his other bed and breakfast in Chelmsford Road. Gary was seven years older than me, prematurely balding, and had spent much of his adult life travelling around Britain with his guitar, whereas I only really knew London. We got on very well and I was fascinated by the stories he told me as we played pool in the local pubs. The trouble with Gary, I used to think, was that when he ran away and got to where he was going, he was still there at the place he'd left.

Soon after I'd moved to Chelmsford Road, Waltham Forest Council gave me a one-bedroom flat on the second floor of a low-rise block on the Cathall Road Estate in Leytonstone. Gary also got a flat, on the Beaumont Estate in Leyton.

Like many estates in east London, Cathall Road had its problems, but because I was a big bloke – and by then I also had a Doberman dog called Masai – I was never given any hassle.

Gary and I began selling furniture out of his battered old van. We'd often tell people the stuff was nicked, even if it wasn't. We spent much of our time, and money, in The Crown, a real pool-players' pub in Leytonstone High Road. When we weren't playing pool or cards, we'd stand at the horseshoe bar chatting with characters such as Welsh John, Irish Tom, a one-eyed Italian called Bruno whom we nicknamed Patch, and Scotch John.

Around this time I began having an affair with Sharon, whose husband was inside for an armed raid on a bingo hall. For me, Sharon was just a bit of added spice in my life. What her husband didn't know wouldn't hurt him, I thought. Unlike my relationship with Louise, this one was purely sexual. We just wanted each other's bodies. For her, I was probably just a way of dealing with the loneliness of being a married woman with a husband in prison.

One afternoon, Gary and I went to an office furniture shop in Boundary Road, Walthamstow, to try to sell two filing cabinets we had picked up from a skip. The owner of the shop was Bulldog Smith. When we walked in, he was sitting at the back watching racing on TV. He was a stocky man in his fifties, with a scarred face topped by a trilby hat. I couldn't help noticing that his trousers were too short and his blue cardigan had holes in the sleeves. He looked a tough character, and it was obvious why he was called Bulldog.

As we gingerly approached him with one of the filing cabinets, he looked up and said in a real cockney accent, 'What a load of rubbish. What 'ave you brought me 'ere?'

Feeling awkward and foolish, Gary and I looked at each other and then at the filing cabinets. 'They're in good nick,' I suggested.

Bulldog wasn't impressed. 'You got these from a dump, didn't ya?'

'No,' I replied, unconvincingly.

'Okay, I'll give ya a tenner, and that's it,' said Bulldog with an air of finality, casting his eyes unenthusiastically over the cabinets as he came out from behind his desk.

'Yeah, okay,' I said, trying to sound as if I wasn't interested in the money.

'But I want you to deliver this desk for me,' said Bulldog, pointing to the far side of the shop. 'And if you get any cream gear, come round and we might be able to do some business.' Bulldog, I discovered, had been an associate of the Krays, but he had fallen out with them after the shooting of Jack 'The Hat' McVitie, a friend of his, in a Stoke Newington club in the sixties. Bulldog's scar was the result of getting on the wrong side of the Krays. Afterwards, apparently, Bulldog had gone round to one of their clubs and smashed all the windows. It was claimed that he was the only person ever to get one over on the Krays.

I began delivering furniture for Bulldog and helping out in the shop. We soon became drinking and gambling partners. I would sit with him in the corner, hanging onto his every word, as he fired my imagination with stories and anecdotes about the villains he had met and what the East End used to be like.

I don't think I have ever met a funnier bloke. One afternoon, two men came into the shop with a list of office furniture they wanted. When they started haggling over the price, Bulldog tipped back his trilby and shouted, 'You must be joking!'

'Don't shout at me,' said one of the guys.

'Whose shop is this?' replied Bulldog. 'Do you pay the rent and rates? If I want to shout in my shop, I will shout as much as I like. Now, get out, the pair of you!'

One day, Bulldog introduced me to his son Ray, who was involved in backstage security at some of London's biggest pop concerts. 'Hey, John,' said Ray one evening in the pub, 'how do you fancy helping me out and earning some money?'

'Doing what?'

'Backstage security. You must be about six foot four, and I know you can handle yourself.'

'Yeah, sounds good,' I said. 'Whereabouts, Ray?'

He took a sip from his pint and leaned back on the bar. 'Run for the World at Hyde Park.'

Little did I know then that I would soon not only be rubbing shoulders with pop stars, but I would also find myself sliding into a world where money was no object, girls were readily available and drugs, danger and violence were part of daily life. What was to become important from now on was power and reputation.

Four

Bouncers

As instructed by Ray, I arrived at Hyde Park a few days later and reported for duty, along with another twenty or so tough-looking geezers. Run for the World was being held to raise money for aid to Third World countries. Thousands of people were going to be running around the park, and many top artists, including Sting and Bob Geldof, were to play a concert.

Ray introduced me to Paddy, the Irish guy who ran Cooler Hand Security, and then he gave me a yellow T-shirt and told me to help some of the other security guys unload some chairs from a lorry. Despite being built like tanks, most of the blokes just took one chair at a time.

'Come on, lads, you can do better than that,' called the driver from the cab.

'Well, why don't you get that lazy, fat mate of yours sitting next to you to give a hand?' retorted one of the blokes.

'That's not my mate; that's my wife!' replied the driver indignantly.

A number of double-decker buses were lined up along Park Lane. In front of each one was a stall selling Run for the World T-shirts for a fiver. One of our jobs was to make sure no one nicked the money. When he discovered that only fifty pence from the sale of each T-shirt went to Run for the World, Ray suggested to a woman on one of the stalls that it would be a good idea if he loaded some of the T-shirts into his Land Rover and drove around the park to try and sell them more widely. She though this was a great idea. So Ray and I went around the park flogging the T-shirts. We must have sold a

35

couple of hundred. At the end, we had a dozen McDonald's bags full of cash – which we pocketed.

Later on, we spotted three guys nicking T-shirts. We grabbed hold of them, dragged them behind some trees and gave them a good hiding. As I pounded one of the blokes with my fists, I remember being exhilarated by the sense of power I felt.

The first major pop concert I worked at was a joint gig by Queen and Status Quo at Wembley Stadium in, I think, the summer of 1984. I met up with Ray at one of the gates at the rear of the stadium. He told me I would be working on the back door between the main stadium and the backstage area, which was under the stand. Given the reputation and following of the two bands, the gig was a sell-out and had attracted a wide cross-section of people – not just the predictable long-haired heavy rockers in their leathers.

At such a huge venue, security was well organised. We weren't expecting any trouble, but we were anticipating that some of the fans might become over-enthusiastic. This nearly always happens at rock concerts, especially if people are fuelled with drink or drugs, or a combination of the two.

I took up my position at the back door, mentally preparing myself for a long, boring afternoon. I was just a body. After a few minutes one of the Wembley staff, an officious little man, told me I was not to let anyone in unless they had the official laminated pass. As if I didn't know that already, I thought, doing my best to ignore him. These passes were like gold dust. It wasn't long before a steady stream of people were coming up to me and asking if they could get in. On each occasion I shook my head and gave them my best you-must-be-joking-mate look. Still, I couldn't fault them for trying. I would have done the same thing.

Then this character in an expensive-looking suit appeared. He needed to get through, he told me, but Queen's lead singer Freddie Mercury had his passes.

'I'm sorry, mate. You can't come in without a pass,' I replied flatly, thinking, 'Go on, pull the other one.' But I had to give him ten out of ten for cheek.

'Yes, but Freddie Mercury has got my passes. I've just told you that.'

'Well, mate. It's catch-22, then, isn't it?' I said nonchalantly.

He shook his head and gave a look of exasperation. 'Look, come over here,' he said, looking furtively around. 'Come here.'

I moved a few feet to the side, still keeping my eye on the door.

'If I bung you a nifty,' he said, lowering his voice, 'then will you let me in?'

'No problem at all,' I replied. Now he was talking my language. He slipped some notes into the palm of my hand, and walked on through.

The next minute, Paddy the boss was standing next to me. 'How much did he give you, John?'

'What are you talking about?' I replied, trying to appear innocent. Paddy was no mug, though.

'That flash geezer. Come on. How much?'

There was no point in lying to Paddy. He'd seen me. 'Fifty quid,' I replied, holding out the money.

'Well, that's good,' grinned Paddy. 'I wouldn't like to think you were doing it for tenners.'

I felt quite good as I left the stadium after the concert. Not only had I been paid thirty-five pounds for the afternoon, but I had also earned a very easy extra fifty quid.

The following week, I was sent with five other guys on an intensive martial arts training course at a house in the Yorkshire countryside. It was led by Len, a former SAS soldier, a small guy with a pot belly and a missing ear. He used to fight for money in Thailand, until one night in a bar someone cut off his ear.

Amongst other things, Len taught us the pressure points of the human body and how to deal with knife and gun attacks. When we practised disarming someone with a knife it was quite painful, because the knife had a cocktail stick taped to the end. We all ended up with lots of pinpricks on our arms and chests. Since coming out of Kidlington, I had often carried a knife with me, but now I decided I should always be tooled up. We also did weight training, went for long runs and learned tai jitsu, which combined kung fu, ninja, karate, boxing and judo. Most martial arts are defence; this type was most definitely attack.

I remember Len telling us that everyone had a sixth sense. He demonstrated this one afternoon by inviting one of his young trainee teachers to come up behind him and attack him with a samurai sword. As soon as the kid lifted the sword, Len swung round and, in a split second, pinned his 'attacker' to the floor with the sword across his throat.

Over the next few months I worked at a number of sell-out concerts, such as Simply Red, Michael Jackson and Bruce Springsteen, as well as boxing tournaments at the Royal Albert Hall. I particularly enjoyed doing the security for a Prince concert at Wembley Arena. The money wasn't brilliant – but there were lots of attractive, half-naked women on stage. The best concert I worked at was Frank Sinatra, who was appearing with Sammy Davis Junior at the Royal Albert Hall. I had specifically asked Brendan if I could work at this concert, as I had always been a big fan of Sinatra. Listening to him croon his way through all those great songs, including, of course, 'My Way', was fantastic.

In security work, you are always thinking of ways to make a few extra quid. I once made a fortune at an Amnesty International concert by selling press passes. It turned out that hardly any press had made use of the special enclosure which had been set aside for them, so a few of us thought we could safely make a few quid on the side. Given the demand for seats at the event, we had no trouble selling the press passes to people outside the stadium. With tickets generally selling at around two hundred pounds, we had no trouble in selling the passes for anything up to a hundred pounds.

John as a baby

John aged four

John aged eight

John with his mum and step dad,
who gave him his first bible

John at home on a night off from supplying

John partying in the East End

John (back row, first from right) with the Franciscan
Friars at the renewal in New York

John in Ireland

John with his dad

John in 2002

John signing the contract with John Toone of Xt3

John with writer Greg Watts

John's Mum and brother David at his book launch
in The Blind Beggar Pub December 2004

John in London's West End

When I left the stadium that evening, I had over a thousand pounds in my pocket.

I was soon learning how to pull off a variety of scams. For example, I used to buy loads of Texas Homecare gift vouchers from a guy at the gym. I never knew if they were genuine or forgeries. It worked like this: I would buy a hundred pounds' worth of vouchers for ten quid, and then go to a Texas Homecare branch and buy expensive items such as drills. I would then return to the store and say something like, 'My wife has already bought me a drill. Can I have my money back?' Without fail, they would always give me a full cash refund. I did this for a couple of months and would drive to Texas branches all over the country, sometimes staying overnight in hotels.

Another scam was with milk tokens. I used to buy about five thousand pounds' worth for forty quid. You couldn't get cash for them, but shops would give you cigarettes instead. I think many of the shopkeepers suspected the tokens were dodgy, but they weren't bothered so long as they were getting their money.

One day, Brendan from Rock Security offered me some door work at Bertie's, a busy restaurant on Charing Cross Road. I was over the moon. It offered better money and, I was told, this was the route to really big bucks – if, that is, you got into the drug dealing. I soon settled into my new role as a doorman, and quickly learned about ways to make extra money. It was easy, for instance, to charge a customer a tenner so that he or she could jump the queue.

After a few months, I was offered a job at Starlight, a popular pub in Chingford, Essex. The pub had seen a few stabbings and Martin, the manager, whom I knew from his days running The Green Man in Leytonstone, was anxious to snuff out the troublemakers. If the pub got a reputation as a violent place, people would stop going there. He had asked Brendan to provide some muscle.

I was asked to work Friday, Saturday and Sunday nights,

and it paid well. The place attracted both the East End boys and the Essex boys. Most were just out for a good night, but some were looking to cause trouble.

Martin told me that his best doorman, Ron, who was about six foot six, had left to work at Sensations. One night, he said, a bloke had pulled out a shotgun in the middle of the pub. Ron just went for him and beat him black and blue. Martin asked me how I thought the trouble could be stopped.

'Simple, Martin,' I replied. 'Over-twenty-ones only, and no trainers and jeans.'

'Well, I think jeans might be going a bit far,' he said, 'but I'm willing to limit admission to over-twenty-ones and ban trainers.'

The first night passed without incident, and I turned several people away for wearing trainers. On the second night a well-dressed man tried to enter the pub, but I refused him entry because of his trainers.

'I'm a friend of Larry's,' he replied. Larry was the owner.

'I'm not bothered. You're not coming in,' I said.

'Go and get Larry,' he demanded.

'Sorry, mate, I'm not leaving here.'

The man insisted I fetch the owner, but I stood my ground. A few minutes later a punter came out. I asked him to go back in and get Larry. When Larry came out, he let the geezer in immediately, because he was a good spender. Later on, I told Martin that I was packing the job in because my authority had been undermined. If I refused admission to one person because they were wearing trainers, and they returned later in shoes and saw someone else at the bar wearing trainers, then they were going to get the hump and probably cause grief. Martin explained the situation to Larry, who gave a pair of shoes to the guy he'd let in.

One night, a rowdy football team turned up. I noticed that two of them were wearing trainers. I explained the pub's policy over trainers, and also said that we didn't admit more than four guys together. A few of the team began to get mouthy. They knew they could overpower me, but even if they did force their way in, they wouldn't get served. It was going to kick off any minute, I thought.

All of a sudden, they went quiet. I looked behind me to see Martin, a guy called Short Arm Bob and eight other regulars standing there, all tooled up with snooker cues and sticks. The football team slunk back into the night.

During my year at Starlight there was one guy who really used to annoy me. Since he was friends with Larry, he thought he had the right to carry on drinking after closing time and be abusive to me when I asked him to leave. On my last night at the pub, I walked over to him and asked him to drink up. I knew exactly what his reaction would be. This time I wasn't going to stand for it, so I took him outside and gave him a right battering.

After I left Starlight, I got a job on the doors at Tango's, a nightclub next to Bertie's. I got on well with Phil, one of the other doormen there. He was a small Irish bloke with dark hair, a good-looking guy who always managed to look scruffy in a suit. He used to drink pints of Guinness like a fish. Although he was married with three kids, he spent little time at his home in Canning Town. He had a string of girlfriends. I soon learned that Phil had no fear of anyone and, like me, he always carried a knife. 'All the public are vermin,' he told me angrily one day. One of the doormen at Bertie's used to annoy Phil by constantly asking us to help sort out trouble at the restaurant. One night, Phil flipped and gave him a pasting in the alley. After that, he never hassled us again.

After a few months at Tango's, I was having a drink and a laugh with Phil in The Boleyn in West Ham, and I mentioned a real hard geezer I had met the week before. 'Yeah, well,' said Phil, 'I've met a lot of people with reputations, but it counts for nothing when they're lying in the gutter with a knife in their back.'

'What do you mean?'

41

'I don't think you know who I am and who I'm involved with.'

He then went on to recount what had happened one night in an East Ham pub. It all revolved around a guy called Daly, who ran a clip joint or speeler, an illegal drinking and gambling den, around the corner from a pub run by Jim Sutton. Jim had taken on the pub after quitting his job as head doorman at Sensations nightclub in the West End, although he later went back to work there. Everyone who used the speeler also used to drink at Jim's pub, which was called Arkwright's because it was open all hours. Daly wasn't happy about this and felt Jim was damaging his business, so one night he decided to go round to the pub to warn Jim off.

Phil had been in the pub having a quick drink with Jim and two other blokes, Ron and Bob, before going to work at Sensations. The pub was packed. Then Daly and five geezers walked in, went straight up to the bar and demanded to know who Jim was.

'I'm him,' said Jim.

'Well, we've come to cut your head off,' said Daly, whipping out a machete.

Jim pulled out a gun from under the bar and shot the guy in the chest.

The place exploded into violence. Phil stabbed Daly in the throat, while Jim ended up being stabbed six times. Bob and Ron were slashed across the face. Phil then pointed the gun at the head of another geezer.

'Leave me. I'm dead!' cried the bloke.

'You are now,' said Phil, and he pulled the trigger. The gun wouldn't fire, so he stabbed him in the head instead. I will never forget the viciousness in Phil's voice as he recounted this incident.

Immediately afterwards, Jim was driven round to a safe house, where a doctor stitched him up. Soon after that, knowing that the police were hunting for them, Jim, Bob and Ron legged it to Spain. Phil refused to go with them because he wanted to stay with his dad, who was critically ill. Eventually Jim, Bob and Ron were arrested in Spain and brought back to London. Phil gave himself up. Sherwin, the same solicitor who had got me off the fraud charges, told them that he could get them off if they paid enough money.

The only evidence the police had against the three of them came from two girls who were looking in through the pub window at the time of the fight. None of the customers present came forward. The girls told the police that they had seen the man behind the bar shoot one man and Phil stab another. Those girls never appeared in court. They were visited, as they say in the East End – meaning they were threatened that if they gave evidence, they would have to suffer the consequences. The cases against all four men were thrown out of court at committal. As I listened to Phil's story, I realised that the man called Ron was the same guy who had worked at Starlight before I arrived.

At the end of a working night, I would usually go on to another nightclub with Phil. We were always treated with respect and given free drinks. It was great. When Jim Sutton returned to Sensations as head doorman, we often went there. I was never that impressed by Sensations. Sure, it was classy, full of wealthy and attractive people, but it wasn't my scene. I liked Jim from the outset, though. I had never seen anyone so confident. He was about six foot tall and, with his neat moustache, he reminded me of Errol Flynn. Although he was polite and charming, I could tell he was a very tough character.

Top bands such as the Pogues and the Tom Tom Club used to play at Tango's. Bob Dylan even did a special gig there one night and Kiss FM, which was then still a pirate radio station, used to host Friday nights. These gigs were always sold out. Unknown to the owner, we earned extra money by reselling tickets. On Monday and Tuesday nights, which were quiet by comparison, we charged punters five quid instead of four, and pocketed the difference. We would usually leave with an extra hundred pounds each.

Looking to make bigger money, Phil and I planned to break into Bertie's. We figured that at the end of a busy weekend there could be anything between twenty and a hundred thousand pounds in the safe.

'It'll be a piece of cake,' claimed Phil.

A few days later, in the middle of the night, we drove over to the West End in my Mercedes. In the back we had a trolley onto which we planned to load the safe. We also had some cutting gear in case we were unable to lift it. We parked in the alleyway beside the restaurant and took the trolley out of the Merc. Using a crowbar, Phil began to force open the door.

Suddenly, we were staring the manager in the face. 'What are you two doing here?' he asked, clearly taken aback.

'Er, we've just come for a late drink,' I replied, unconvincingly. What was he still doing here after the restaurant had closed?

'So what's all this gear and that trolley for, then?'

We just turned around, got back into the Merc and drove off. As we made our way back to east London, we were worried. If we got nicked, we could be facing a prison stretch. The only thing in our favour was that the manager only knew us as 'John' and 'Phil' and that we worked for Brendan and Warren's security company.

The next morning, we phoned the boss and told him we needed to see him urgently. He invited us round to his house in Ladbroke Grove. We told him that the restaurant manager, mistakenly, thought we were planning to rob Bertie's and the police might contact him. 'Listen,' I said, 'we need you to lose those index cards with our details on.'

'I don't know if I can do that,' he answered. 'I don't want any grief from the coppers.'

'Well, put it this way,' said Phil, putting a knife to his throat, 'if you don't, you'll get more from me. I'll cut your throat.'

He knew Phil wasn't joking. He went upstairs to his office, returned with the cards and handed them to Phil.

There was still the problem of the manager at Bertie's. He needed a visit. The next night Alex, a mate of Phil's and mine, turned up and, as they say, had a word with him. We never heard anything from the police.

We both got nicked a few months later, though, after we beat up a punter at Tango's. He was a lippy geezer and was making a nuisance of himself. When I asked him to leave, he refused and started getting violent. Phil and I slung him out, dragged him into the alley and gave him a right pasting. He phoned the police later, and we were arrested and charged with actual bodily harm.

The case never came to court. Jim made sure of that. He found out who the bloke was and discovered that he owned a car showroom in south-east London. One night shortly after that, there was a break-in at the showroom. Nothing was nicked. Instead, a brick and a can of petrol were placed on every car. A note was left for the owner. It said, 'This is Mr Brick. If anyone appears in court over the case of Phil and John, then Mr Brick will be placed inside the car and the petrol will be poured around the showroom. It will be a wonderful bonfire.'

By now, I knew Jim very well and had become part of his 'firm'. I remember one day he asked Phil, Ron and me to go to a pub in West Ham to help him sort out a bit of business with a south London face. 'And, John, you'll need to wear a black suit and a black tie,' he added.

When I arrived at the pub, I was amazed at what I saw. There must have been over sixty geezers wearing black suits and ties crowded around the bar. To get an army like this together, Jim must have had a lot of respect. A few minutes later, in walked the south London geezer and half a dozen blokes. I wished I had a camera to capture the look on their faces when they saw us all. I reckoned the guy had come thinking he was going to tell Jim where to go. He and Jim disappeared into a back room. I don't know what was said, but when they came out Jim was smiling and the other bloke wasn't.

One night, Lenny McLean, a notorious bare-knuckle fighter who went on to write a book about his exploits, sent some muppet around to Sensations to tell Jim that Lenny was coming to the club later on and wanted champagne and red-carpet treatment. Jim was unimpressed. If Lenny came to the club, he said, he paid like everyone else.

I had met Lenny on a couple of occasions at the British Oak pub on Lea Bridge Road when I was out with Bulldog, who used to help run unlicensed boxing bouts. I didn't like Lenny. He was very aggressive, a bit of a bully, and had little respect for anyone, although he respected Bulldog. While Lenny was known to be a great fighter, he never carried a gun or a knife. In that respect, he wasn't really a face. In the old days he would have been, but once guns came on the scene, people like Lenny were seen as small-timers.

Anyway, on the night in question, Lenny arrived at Sensations shortly after he'd sent his messenger round, just as Jim had expected. Jim asked Lenny to walk with him into an alley by the club. Before Lenny could say anything, Jim produced a gun and told him that he wasn't dealing with boxers now but real chaps. Stunned, Lenny just turned around and walked away.

Violence, or the possibility of it, was becoming part of my life. I began carrying a machete and a bottle of CS gas in my car. I never carried them on the door, though. Instead I carried a bowie knife, a lemon Jiffy container filled with ammonia, and sometimes a knuckle-duster. Although I was six foot four, there was always someone who would want to pick a fight with me. You always have to watch your back.

As a doorman, I became very good at judging people from their body language. If anyone appeared aggressive, I wouldn't let them in. I developed an instinct for those who were going to cause aggro and those who were just a bit boisterous. I remember once at the West End pub Nightingales, a big black guy in a vest and with enormous arms turned up with his girlfriend. He was very cocky and I told him I wasn't letting him in.

'Why?' he protested.

'Because you're not dressed right.'

'What do you mean, I'm not dressed right? Why?' he said, pointing his finger at me.

I kept silent, refusing to get drawn into an argument. I had told him he wasn't coming in, and that was the end of the matter.

'So are you going to stop me?' he persisted.

'No, but he is.' As I spoke, another of the doormen floored the guy with a single punch. His girlfriend began screaming and shouting at us, but we just stood there and let her sound off. After a couple of minutes, the guy pulled himself up and slunk off as quietly as a mouse.

My most memorable night as a doorman was the time when about twenty rugby players turned up at Nightingales. They were all very smart in their blazers, ties and slacks and assured us they wouldn't cause any trouble. They seemed okay, so the head doorman agreed they could come in, but he explained that they all had to leave bang on 11 p.m. In other words, there was no extra drinking-up time. They said that was fine, and settled down in the upstairs bar. The upstairs bar attracted all the tourists, while downstairs drug dealing used to take place. The manager knew about the dealing and was given a generous cut from the proceeds.

At closing time I went up to one of the rugby team and asked him to drink up. 'We've got twenty minutes,' he said dismissively.

'No. You were all told when you came in that there's no drinking-up time.' He swore at me and took a sip from his pint. 'I'll be back in one minute and I want you out then,' I said.

I could see trouble on the cards here, so I went downstairs to warn two of the other doormen, who were clearing out the punters. They came upstairs with me and we all took up strategic positions around the bar.

Then I went over to the same rugby player and told him to leave. He swore at me again. That was it. I knocked his drink out of his hand. 'You're a nutter,' he said, turning on me.

'That's right. I'm a nutter,' I replied, grabbing him by the blazer and marching him towards the door. Within a couple of minutes, we had lobbed them all out of the pub and locked the doors. It was an incredible piece of professionalism.

On another occasion, I went up to a guy and asked him to leave because he had been making a nuisance of himself on the dance floor with some of the women. He walked towards the door, then turned round waving a knife. I went ballistic and went for him, but he turned and fled.

As I began to establish myself as a doorman, I was offered work at countless clubs, including Buzz Bar, Cairos and Driver's in the West End, The Farley in Stoke Newington, and Kitson's in Limehouse. The only time I was ever hit was at Driver's, when a geezer punched me in the eye. One of his mates had to put me in an arm lock, as I would probably have killed the bloke. I came close to getting hit one other time, too – by a woman. I had lobbed a Moroccan bloke out of the club after I caught him leaning over the bar to fill his pint glass. Then I spotted his girlfriend, who weighed about twenty-two stone, storming angrily across the dance floor towards me. Oh no, I thought. 'If you come any nearer, I'm going to knock you spark out,' I warned her. To my relief, she went away. To have to defend yourself against a woman – especially a twenty-two stone one – is every doorman's nightmare.

Most of the doormen I knew were real villains, but there was a mutual respect amongst doormen for each other, although little for anyone else, especially the police. Compared to soldiers, some people think doormen aren't that hard. One night I asked my stepbrother Simon and three of his mates, who were all in the Grenadier Guards, to help me out on the door at Nightingales. They were all over six foot tall and very physically fit, but halfway through the night they said they'd had enough of the aggro and were going home. 'It's like world war three,' Simon said.

At Driver's, in Covent Garden, we wore bomber jackets and trousers instead of suits, because there were so many fights there. The club, which was open until 3 a.m., had no dress code, so it attracted all sorts. One night, a girl and her boyfriend were badly beaten up in the street after they had left the club. They weren't troublemakers, just out for a good night. Apparently, one of the guys who beat them up hadn't liked the fact that the girl wouldn't dance with him. Phil, who had come to the club for a drink, was as incensed as I was, so we got in my car and went looking for the guys. From the description the couple had given us, we knew what they looked like. We had clocked them fooling around earlier in the evening.

We figured there would be a good chance that they were waiting for a night bus in Trafalgar Square. We drove around the square a couple of times and then, sure enough, we spotted them sitting on a wall. They were laughing. We pulled up, leapt out of the car and, ignoring the crowds waiting for buses, went for them. The taller one scarpered and Phil went after him. I caught the other one, put him up against the wall and began laying into him. Suddenly, I heard screaming. I looked over my shoulder to see Phil furiously stabbing the legs of the guy he had caught.

The following night when I turned up at Driver's, the owner told me that a doorman from another club was looking for Phil and me. It turned out that the two guys we had beaten up were friends of his. Phil and I went straight round to see this doorman. By the time we reached the club, Phil was ready to explode. He went up to the doorman, pulled out a gun and said, 'Have you got a problem with us? After what those two did to that couple, it's a good job we didn't skin them alive.' The doorman was terrified and said he didn't even know the two guys.

Some people I threw out would vow to return with a gun, but they never did. I did hear about some doormen who got shot, though. Usually this was because they had given someone a real kicking. I remember this happened once to a doorman at a club in Limehouse. It was the silent guys you really had to worry about.

I never really had any fear on the door, because I knew I had back-up from the other guys, and we had a range of weapons inside the club to deal with any troublemakers. Without a doubt, the best doorman I ever worked with was Max, a six foot two Italian weightlifter. Max appeared very professional and laid-back, and he was extremely polite to the punters. There was something about him that commanded instant respect, though. If you messed him about, that was it. I once saw him carry a US Marine out by the throat.

I was now finding myself investing the money I made in drugs. On one occasion, Phil and I were buying two kilos of rocky from a little firm in Brixton that someone had told us about. They tried to con us into thinking that they were giving us class rocky when, in fact, it tasted like filth. When we refused to pay, they started to get aggressive. Suddenly, Phil pulled out a gun and pointed it at them. They froze, terrified. Then one of them pointed to a bag containing the good gear. We bought a couple of kilos, threw the money on the table, and left. I discovered that with an investment of between one and a half and two thousand pounds for a kilo of dope, we could double our money by getting people to sell it on in ounces. This was to lead me into a greater involvement in the whole drugs scene.

Five

The drug scene

I WAS CHATTING WITH Jim late one night in a bar when he told me he had received a tip-off that there were forty kilos of dope in a railway arch lock-up in Hackney, and that the people who owned the dope were nobodies. Had it been some firm, not amateurs, who had the dope, then Jim wouldn't have touched it. He was smart.

'Fancy giving me and Phil a hand, John?' he asked.

'Yeah, sounds tasty, Jim,' I replied, thinking I would be in for a good cut here.

A few nights later Jim, Phil and I drove over to Hackney. We parked the van a few yards from the lock-up, in a deserted back street, and scanned the area. All was quiet apart from the sound of the traffic on the main road. Using a pair of bolt cutters, we bust the lock on the door, eased our way in and shone our torches around. The dope – rocky – was in several crates in one corner. Working quickly, we took it out of the crates, placed it in black bin liners, loaded it into the van and drove to Jim's house near Chigwell in Essex. Jim lived in style: the house was set in several acres of garden and had a swimming pool at the rear. He gave me ten kilos as my cut. I knew I would have no trouble selling it to the dealers on the Cathall Road Estate.

Jim then drove Phil and me to Leyton, where I stored the dope in the old, beaten-up Rover I kept outside my flat. I never drove it, as I had a BMW and a Mercedes as well. I just used it for storing anything dodgy.

It's a small world when you're a criminal. You soon get to know or hear about those who move in criminal circles. The following night, I went to a local pub to meet Pep, a dealer I knew quite well. I sold him two kilos for three and a half thousand pounds, and told him to put the word around the estate. Within a few days I had sold it all and pocketed around fifteen thousand pounds. I had never earned such easy money.

Soon after that, Jim asked me to collect a Land Rover from a car park at Folkestone and drive it up to Liverpool. He gave me ten thousand quid for the job, so I knew the Land Rover must have been packed with cocaine, or possibly even gold – but it wasn't my job to ask questions.

By the late 1980s, the London drug scene had become very international. Two guys who were heavily into that scene were Syed, an Iraqi, and Afif, a Palestinian with connections to the Palestinian Liberation Organisation. I used to buy blank credit cards from Afif, who would get them from bent postmen. It usually took four days for the cards to be cancelled. By this time, you could have spent up to five thousand pounds.

Syed, who had deserted the Iraqi army after killing an officer, was a doorman, very well respected and loyal. He was a stocky bloke who always had a smile on his face and loved inviting people to his house for six-course Arab meals. He was a great backgammon player, too. Afif, who looked a little bit like Omar Sharif, was only interested in making money out of people, and would stab you in the back without a second thought. He was constantly wining and dining me, in the hope that I would introduce him to people like Jim and Bulldog. There was no way I would ever have done that.

Through Syed and Afif, I met many millionaire Arabs, often in restaurants in Bayswater and on the Edgware Road. They liked having contact with London villains. Once I was asked to help with security at a birthday party, in a top West End hotel, for the daughter of a Kuwaiti businessman. Several hundred people turned up, including a number of high-class prostitutes. One guy there started causing trouble, so I marched him out of the hotel in a stranglehold, took him into the alley around the side and gave him a few slaps. At the end of the night, the Kuwaiti host thanked me for dealing with the incident and gave me an extra two and a half grand.

One day, Afif told me he had eight hijacked lorries full of electrical items. They had, apparently, been hidden in a garage in Kilburn and a warehouse in Wembley. He asked me if I could use my contacts to set up a meeting with two top south London faces. Against my better judgement, I agreed to do this.

We met at the Hilton Hotel in Park Lane, where the south London faces had booked a suite for the morning. Over a champagne breakfast we discussed the deal. The geezers said they wouldn't buy eight lorries unless they had a list of the items they contained. Afif didn't seem to know exactly what was in the lorries. He talked vaguely about videos, camcorders and so on. In addition, he didn't seem to know if there were, in fact, eight lorries. I remember thinking that my credibility was disappearing fast. Why hadn't Afif bothered to find out the details? I could see from the faces of the south London villains that they were getting more and more frustrated with Afif.

Afif then said he would take them to the lorries so that they could see for themselves. The geezers didn't want to go there. When Afif kept on insisting that they go, and that they give him forty thousand pounds, the atmosphere became very tense.

'Listen, Afif, they don't want to go to the lorries,' I interrupted, getting annoyed. Turning to the two geezers, I apologised for wasting their time. I then made a point of leaving the hotel on my own, and vowed never to have anything to do with Afif again. Later, I discovered from Syed that Afif's plan had been to take the geezers to the lorries, take their money and then shoot them. Whether Afif had been planning to shoot me as well, I will never know.

With their reputation for drug dealing, shootings and murder, the Yardies – Jamaican gangsters – have made their mark in the London underworld during the last twenty years. I never really came across them, but I do remember when they moved into Hackney. The local firms didn't like to see these Jamaicans on their manor, so they sent someone round to a Yardie house to tell them they weren't welcome. One of the Yardies pulled out a sub-machine-gun, put it up against the nostril of the man and told him that was their response. Later that night, four Yardies were shot and their house was set alight. They left.

A mate of Syed's, Terry, began to supply me with cocaine, while a character called Double Duster (he got the name because he used to fight with two knuckle-dusters) supplied me with sulphate or cannabis. Apart from making money from drug deals, I also used the gear myself to blot out my conscience.

Cannabis could be obtained as resin, a liquid form, grass, which you rolled, or rocky and leb, which you burned, crumbled and then smoked. The worst type of cannabis was black, made from the pulp of the plant. Cocaine, on the other hand, came in only two types: powder, which was usually mixed with things such as baby milk or laxative, and which you sniffed, or crack, the purest form. To produce crack you heated the cocaine and then, when it had crystallised, you had a rock left. Crack would be smoked through a pipe, or by sucking a straw attached to a bottle which was full of water and covered by silver paper with holes in.

I once visited a crack factory in a house in Battersea. Usually crack factories were located on a farm or in a warehouse in the middle of the countryside, not in inner London. The house was like a fortress. To get in you had to go through four reinforced steel doors. The factory was located in the basement, where some young women washed the crack. In case of a police raid, a secret tunnel, which you entered through a trapdoor, connected the house with another house across the road.

Sulphate and ecstasy were very popular drugs with those

on the rave scene. Sulphate, or speed as it was sometimes known, could be taken in two ways, either by injecting or snorting it. Sulphate gave you a lot of energy and allowed you to stay awake for long periods, but coming down off it was not very pleasant. I never liked it. Ecstasy, which came in tablet form, was very similar. It gave you a lot of energy, but also created a very mellow feeling. You not only felt that you wanted to dance, but you also felt very sexually aroused.

Occasionally, undercover police officers would enter the clubs looking for drugs. Guys like Jim, however, had close contacts with certain police officers and they would obtain lists of where and when the surveillance was planned. For passing on the information, those police officers would receive a bung. We would then make sure that there were no drugs or deals happening on a night when the club was under surveillance. Sometimes we didn't have the precise day, only the week, but we would still make sure there was no drug activity. If drugs were found, then the club could be closed down. I don't ever recall anyone being arrested for drugs offences at any of the pubs or clubs at which I worked.

I soon built up a contact book containing the names and phone numbers of drug suppliers and dealers. I was simply the middleman. I never had an address for my contacts, only a phone number. A dealer would phone me and ask for, say, an ounce of crack. I would then phone up a supplier, get a price and arrange for the two parties to meet somewhere, usually in a multi-storey or supermarket car park. This was before the advent of CCTV. The supplier never went to these meetings himself; he would send an errand boy. After the deal had been done, I would meet the supplier in a pub and get my cut of the money, in a brown envelope. For example, if the cocaine was £1,100 an ounce, the dealer would pay the supplier £1,400, and I would make £300.

A dealer who bought an ounce of pure cocaine for £1,400 knew that he was going to make a massive profit by mixing the cocaine with baby milk powder or something similar to spread it around more. The less you cut it, the more people wanted it, because it meant they could cut it themselves and sell it on. The further down the chain it went, the worse the quality became. People used to come to me to buy drugs because they knew I had good connections around London, the gear was always quality and, unlike some characters, I never ripped anyone off. It's when people start ripping other people off that the drug wars start.

The first time I tried cocaine was when I was working at a Kensington nightclub. A lot of dealers paid us well in order to operate there. Three of us worked downstairs in the club, and six guys worked upstairs. The guys upstairs confiscated the drugs as people came in, while those of us downstairs looked for people behaving suspiciously. We often went into the gents, where we would stand on the toilet bowl of one cubicle and look over into the òther. If we saw a bloke not doing his business, so to speak, one of us would bang on the door. Unaware that he was being watched from the next cubicle, the guy would usually stuff the drugs down his under-wear. When he emerged he would deny having any drugs. We would tell him we had seen him concealing them and then give him the option of either giving the drugs to us or being handed over to the police. The drugs were always given to us. We would tell the punter we would flush the drugs down the toilet, but of course we never did. At the end of the night we would often have a couple of thousand pounds worth of drugs. Back then, coke was selling at fifty quid for a gram, while ecstasy tablets used to sell for a tenner.

I also began attending crack parties at Syed's flat in Notting Hill Gate. We would have a meal with champagne and then afterwards smoke about a thousand pounds worth of crack between us. We would usually end up having sex with prosti-tutes or girls we had picked up at one of the clubs. A party could go on for two days.

A hit from crack lasts between two and four minutes, during which time you feel euphoric. Think of the greatest joy you have ever felt and multiply this by a thousand, and you have the buzz that crack gives you. Crack also makes you feel superhuman and you have no conscience about anything. It makes you paranoid, however, and you only care about the crack. You don't care about yourself or anyone else. It's the most addictive drug there is, even more so than heroin. I never dealt in heroin, though. This was because the people I associated with believed that heroin only brought about misery. It was a sort of code of ethics, albeit a false one. Like cocaine, cannabis makes you paranoid, but it also makes you lethargic and often leads to heavy drinking as you try to combat the paranoia. Even though cannabis itself isn't addictive, the buzz it gives you is. In my experience, you soon get bored with one kind of drug and eventually will want to try others.

By now I was becoming a successful 'businessman' through my drug dealing. I decided to rent a second flat, on the Beaumont Estate close to Cathall Road, so that it would be more difficult for the police to find me. With so much money coming in from my drug deals, I also decided to rent a luxury, £520-per-week penthouse in a St John's Wood mansion block overlooking Lord's cricket ground. I felt I needed a salubrious place where I could do certain deals – and also where I could take girlfriends. At that time, I was often seeing two or three girls simultaneously. Only my closest associates knew where this flat was, however.

I spent money like water. I would think nothing of going to Oxford Street and spending five hundred pounds on clothes. I used to eat in top restaurants and stay in the best hotels, and never bothered to look at the prices. One weekend, I took a girl I had picked up at Driver's to Brighton and we stayed in the plush Queen's Hotel for two nights. We went to restaurants and a casino and enjoyed a shopping spree. The fact that I had spent four thousand pounds in a weekend meant nothing to me. I loved cars, and now I owned a metallic silver BMW Series 7 with a personalised plate – RE 800

(I sometimes called myself Robert Ellis because of this) – and a classic 1970s white Mercedes saloon with immaculate silverwork.

I also drank and gambled away a lot of the money. I would think nothing of spending three hundred quid on a night out. I would spend the afternoons in pubs, at the bookie's, or at Walthamstow, Romford or Hackney dog tracks. I particularly liked pubs such as The Frog and Nightgown on the Old Kent Road and The Rose and Crown in Stratford, where they had live singers. One of the worst things about working as a bouncer was having to listen to all that garage, house, dance and acid music. I couldn't stand it! Interestingly, Bulldog had a very good voice and he sometimes entered pub talent contests to perform his version of Al Jolson singing 'Mammy'.

Away from the criminal world, I used to go and see my dad once a month and my mum a bit more often. With his background in the police, I think my dad guessed I was con-nected with various villains, but he never said anything. Sometimes I would go with him to the bar at West Ham football ground. I was never interested in the football. The bar was just a good place to drink and gamble. My dad had retired from the police after he was injured while on duty at a West Ham football match. A guy had stuck a ripped beer can into his girlfriend's face, and my dad went into the crowd to arrest him. He was jumped on by the guy's mates, who began kicking and beating him. Ironically, a steward jumped in to help my dad, but my dad, not realising who he was, whacked him with his truncheon and broke his nose.

When I was twenty-six, I met Charlotte – or Charlie, as I called her – at Bulldog's shop. She was always hanging around there. Bulldog told me she had nowhere to live after rowing with her mum. Feeling sorry for her, I told her she could sleep at my flat until she got herself sorted out. The next day she and her three-year-old son Jason moved in with me. It was good having Charlie around, I thought. She kept the flat tidy and would always offer to cook me a meal when I came in.

And Jason was a loveable kid. Charlie and I soon began sleeping together. What she didn't know was that I already had a girlfriend, Angie, whom I had been seeing for a couple of months.

With my 'hard man' image, it was easy to pull girls. When Phil and I were on the pull together, the routine didn't vary much. We never had to chat women up. They always came up to us. At the end of a night, we would often have three or four phone numbers. It was then just a case of picking the girls we most fancied and asking them to wait until everyone else had left. When the club had closed, we would take them on to another club and then head back to my flat for sex. We lost count of the number of women we slept with. It was all about physical gratification, not love. I was selfish, just using women. Even at the time, I never felt good when I woke up the morning after – sometimes next to a girl whose name I couldn't remember.

I shared very little about myself with Charlie, or with anyone else, in those days. I still felt the rejection I had experienced as a child. I wasn't really in touch with who I was, and I was still nursing a lot of anger and bitterness in my heart. Charlie knew no more about me when she left than when she had first moved in. I only really felt close to my dog, Masai.

I gave no thought to the future or to the consequences of my actions, and I was becoming more and more violent. Once, when Phil and I were driving back in the early hours of the morning after a night out in the West End, we got to a set of traffic lights in Barking and I noticed a guy staring at us. I wound the window down and asked him what he was looking at. He swore back at me and sped off. We set off after him and rammed his car from the back. He pulled over. So did we. I slipped a knuckle-duster on and jumped out. The guy sat there in his car looking frightened, but I could see that he had a cosh in his left hand. I punched through the window with the knuckle-duster and smashed him in the side of the face, leaving him spark out, covered with blood and glass. I walked back to our car and said casually to Phil, 'He doesn't look too well.' We drove off, laughing and joking.

Six

Going ballistic

LOOKING BACK, I CAN NOW SEE that I started to become more violent because of the people with whom I was associating. When you're mixing with geezers who have shot and stabbed people, you have to try to match their levels of violence in order to gain their respect. Respect was everything to me in those days. I was proud that I was a member of three firms: Jim's, Bulldog's and Syed's.

I was now involved in what's known as 'debt collecting'. When some people feel they can't achieve justice through the law they will sometimes resort to other, more drastic means. There are always geezers willing to apply a bit of muscle to an individual on their behalf, if the price is right. I was one of those geezers.

Debt collecting could be risky, though. If you paid a visit to someone and told them you would be returning a few days later for the money, you could find the police waiting to arrest you and, if convicted, you would be sent down for demanding money with menaces. To avoid this, I had a rule of only visiting a person once.

The landlord of a pub in Camberwell phoned me once, and asked if I could sort out a spot of bother he was having with some local youths who were demanding free drinks and threatening to smash up the pub. I told the landlord we would need six guys and it would cost five hundred pounds each per night.

'That much!' he exclaimed.

'Yeah, if you want the job done properly,' I told him.

I knew the pub was a place where you could get anything:

black-market cigarettes, nicked videos, fake passports and driving licences, even prostitutes and guns. The 'guvnor' also ran an illegal card school in the basement. If he gave in to the yobs, he would lose his reputation as a face and all this extra business he was involved in. He duly paid up, in advance, as was the normal practice.

The following Friday night, the six of us went to the pub to wait for the yobs. We sat around for three hours, but they didn't show up. We returned on the next three nights, but again there was no sign of the youths. It was costing the landlord three grand a night, so he insisted on cutting our number to three – me, a power-lifter called Roy, and Steve, a kick-boxer who had worked the doors in Thailand.

On the fifth night, the three of us were sitting in the pub when a dozen or so yobs cockily sauntered in, went up to the bar and immediately started hassling the guvnor. He nodded to us. We could tell that the youths were muppets. They were all talk and not up to taking us on, even though there were only three of us.

Roy stood up and walked over to them and, in no uncertain terms, ordered them to leave. They started giving him lip, but Roy, as I knew, had no fear.

'Why should we leave?' sneered one of the group.

'You'll find out in two seconds if you don't,' replied Roy coldly.

Steve and I were now standing behind him. I had my hand on the CS gas canister in my pocket. Suddenly, Steve released a lightning kick and sent the lippy one reeling onto the floor. Roy grabbed another youth by the neck. I took out my CS gas and waved it threateningly at the youths, who began to back away. The lippy one picked himself up off the floor, clutching his stomach.

'Do you all want some, then?' challenged Roy. 'Who's first?'

The youths stood motionless and then, one by one, started to leave the pub.

'And don't you ever come in here again,' shouted Roy after

them, 'because if you do, you'll regret it for the rest of your lives!'

The landlord was so pleased with our night's work that he paid us double rates. He never had any more trouble from the yobs after that.

That sort of job was not so common. It was direct debt collecting that provided me with regular work. With debt collecting we would usually only take on a job that was worth twenty grand or more. We would charge three hundred pounds per day each in expenses, plus twenty per cent of the money recovered. Once we had accepted a job, we guaranteed that we would take no longer than three days to recover the money.

We would always check out with Bulldog and Jim whether the person we were being asked to recover a debt from was 'connected'. We didn't want to go barging into the house of a face. We never seriously beat anyone up, although we did occasionally have to rough them up a little. More often than not, though, they would be terrified enough just by having a machete pointing at their neck.

One time, a second-hand car dealer in Hackney asked Syed and me to recover the twenty-eight grand he was owed by his ex-business partner. He offered us a bonus if we broke the guy's legs. When we went round to the geezer's house in north London, however, we could tell from the state of it that he didn't have two pennies to rub together. He told us that if we were going to beat him up, then we should get it over with.

'I don't have any money and that's the truth,' he pleaded.

We knew it was the truth. There was no way we were going to lump this guy, so we left and never contacted the car dealer again.

Another time, we went to a jeweller to recover twenty thousand pounds owed to another jeweller. When he told us he didn't have that sort of cash, we told him we would take five Rolex watches instead and he could report them stolen. We knew we could sell them for two thousand pounds each.

We went back to the other jeweller and gave him three thousand pounds, plus the grand he had paid us initially. He was happy with this, and we made three grand each from selling the watches. I kept one of them for myself, though.

The same jeweller was owed thirty grand for a batch of Rolex watches he had sold to a Pakistani man. He asked Ted, a bare-knuckle fighter who thought he was another Lenny McLean, to recover the money. Syed and I were to help. I'd met Ted a week before and all he spoke about was himself and fighting. The problem was that he didn't have the charisma to cut it as a real hard man. What's more, he never respected people. I wasn't happy with the way Ted had done the deal, either. Instead of receiving cash upfront, we were to receive thirty per cent of the value of the watches, but only after we had got the money.

Syed, Ted and I drove to Richmond in my Mercedes. Arriving at the address we'd been given, we discovered it was a print works. We went piling in. The men and women standing by their machines looked stunned. Ted stormed across the room, grabbed hold of a stocky guy by his neck and demanded to know where the Pakistani bloke was.

'I don't know him!' spluttered the man.

'Ted!' I called above the noise of the machines.

'Wait, John!' he shouted back. Turning to the petrified bloke he was gripping, he said, 'If you don't tell me where he is, I'm going to take you outside and batter you.'

'Ted!' I shouted again.

'What is it?'

'Let him go. It's the wrong address.' I'd checked the piece of paper with the address written on it that I was carrying in my pocket, and realised that we had turned up not at number 247, but at number 274.

'I'm surrounded by incompetents,' said Ted angrily as we got back into the car and sped off to the correct address.

There was no one there. We asked several neighbours if

they had seen the man, but they all said he hadn't been there for a few days.

Feeling that we had been on a wild goose chase, we decided to drive back to east London. Our mood was glum. We hadn't been paid. To lighten the atmosphere, I wound down the window and put Pavarotti on full blast. I often used to listen to Pavarotti and opera music in the car. I found it relaxing.

As we drove along Battersea Park Road, we were cut up by a red BMW. Ted, who was driving, was incensed and began cursing loudly. When we reached the next set of traffic lights, he deliberately rammed the back of the BMW. Four black guys jumped out, looking as though they meant business – but when we got out and they saw the size of us, they scattered. With our greased-back hair and black suits we looked like something straight out of *The Godfather*. Ted and Syed chased after them, while I started kicking their car to bits, to the soundtrack of Pavarotti.

Eventually we all got back into the Mercedes, feeling much more cheerful. As we were about to pull away, however, a police car appeared and blocked our exit. An officer walked towards us and ordered us to remain in the car and give him the keys. Sirens could be heard in the distance, and suddenly more police cars and vans appeared from nowhere.

Syed and Ted started arguing with the officer. A sergeant came over to speak to me, as I seemed to be the calmest one, and said, 'Look, we can see you're not muppets or anything. Are you a firm?'

'We might be,' I replied with a shrug of the shoulders.

'Well, tell us what happened.'

The four black guys had now reappeared and were standing a few feet away with a group of police officers. I told the sergeant that the other car had cut us up and that one of the black guys had pulled a knife on us. By now, I noticed, there was a tailback of traffic in both directions.

The sergeant went over to the black guys and recommended that they didn't press charges. They didn't. As we drove off,

Ted switched on Capital Radio. We all laughed when we heard a traffic report saying that there was serious congestion in Battersea due to 'an incident'.

Then my mobile phone rang. It was my brother David. 'John,' he said, 'don't forget to be at St Joseph's Church in Leyton at 10 a.m. tomorrow. You're my son's godfather, remember?'

'Of course. How could I forget something like that?' I answered – having, in fact, completely forgotten all about Andrew's baptism.

'Was that Bulldog ringing about that gear in Bermondsey?' asked Syed.

'No,' I laughed. 'It was my brother reminding me to be in church tomorrow!'

I can remember a number of amusing incidents from that time. Once Phil turned up at my flat in Cathall Road at 2.30 a.m. and asked me to go with him to nick a hundred mountain bikes from a lock-up in Dagenham. He hadn't passed his driving test, and when he did drive he was lousy. He loved adventure, however, and I hadn't forgotten that time when we had tried to break into Bertie's.

'We can sell them for fifty quid a time,' he said persuasively.

'Yeah, but how are we going to shift them?' I asked.

'In that,' said Phil, pointing out of the window.

I peered out and, to my astonishment, saw a seven-ton lorry parked down below.

'You're joking!' I exclaimed. 'I've never driven anything that big.'

'There's a first time for everything,' he grinned.

Out of loyalty to Phil I agreed to drive the lorry, but I was soon regretting it. As we drove through Leyton, I partly demolished two lampposts and narrowly missed half a dozen cars and a telephone box. It was like driving a tank. Thank God the streets were deserted, I thought.

Eventually we got to the lock-up and I parked the lorry in front. There were two cars blocking the doors to the lock-up, and Phil and I tried to break into the cars with bolt cutters, so that we could move them. Smashing the windows might have drawn the attention of the people living in the flats across the road. It was no good, though: the bolt cutters wouldn't do the job. Phil then suggested that I get back in the lorry and simply shunt the cars along. I told him it would make too much noise, but he was insistent.

'Why are you so determined to get these mountain bikes?' I asked.

'Because I promised my son one for Christmas,' he replied.

I couldn't believe it. Phil was rolling in money. Why did he want to break into a lock-up?

'Listen, Phil,' I said firmly. 'I'll buy him one. Come on. Let's get out of here before we get nicked.'

In the underworld there is one vital code: you don't grass on someone. This is why so-called 'supergrasses' are given secret addresses and around-the-clock protection by the police. I never grassed anyone up – although I must admit that when I read in the paper that there was a big reward for information leading to the arrest and conviction of someone I didn't like, it was tempting.

I was asked to take part in a few bank robberies, but I always felt that when you weighed up your cut with the possible prison sentence you might get, the risk was too great. I was never a great risk-taker. I was very careful about the type of crime in which I got involved.

I was never asked to act as a hit man. I do, however, recall being in a West End club one night with Phil when he introduced me to a bloke he said was a hit man. The geezer looked like Mr Joe Average. There was nothing about him to suggest that he had killed at least four people, but I remember thinking that there was a real deadness in his eyes.

One day, Bulldog told me that a guy he had sacked from his shop had nicked some fake passports and about two hundred quid. He had sacked the guy because he had been pocketing some of the money from the furniture he sold.

It turned out that the guy had come back one day and let himself in with his spare set of keys. When another of Bulldog's staff arrived, the guy had pulled a knife on him. Bulldog asked me to do the bloke if I saw him.

About a month later, I was sitting in a Walthamstow café having breakfast when I saw the guy going into the DHSS office across the road. I left the café and waited for him to come out. When he did, I hauled him into an alley, grabbed him by the throat, threw him against the wall and punched him a few times in the face. He slumped to the ground and I gave him a hard kick in the head, leaving him groaning and covered in blood.

Two days later I was arrested and charged with actual bodily harm. I denied attacking the guy and claimed I had never heard of him. When I told Phil about it, he set up a false alibi. The story was that Phil, Martin – the manager of Starlight – and I had been playing golf in Epping Forest at the time of the attack. My solicitor Sherwin told me there was no evidence to convict me, so I had nothing to worry about.

When the case came to Walthamstow Magistrates' Court, the guy said that he had worked for Bulldog and that he had been attacked because he had taken some money. When Sherwin cross-examined him, the guy said the attack was so vicious that everything about it was etched in his mind.

'Really?' said Sherwin. 'In that case, why is it that you told the police the attack took place in the morning and yet you just told me it took place in the afternoon?'

When Bulldog's son Ray was called to give evidence, he said that he was the owner of the shop and that the guy had never worked for him. That was it. The case was thrown out. A couple of weeks later, I heard that the guy had had both his legs broken in an attack by someone with a baseball bat. I suspected Phil had probably had something to do with that.

One day Ted phoned me and asked if I would go and see him at his house in Kingston. He said he'd got into a ruck with a doorman at Options nightclub, and the doorman was out to get him. It sounded a bit of a half-baked story, but I agreed to go and see him. I took Syed with me.

When Ted opened the door and ushered us into the living room, he seemed a bit edgy. Ray and a few other guys were already sitting there. We all listened as Ted told us about the fight. 'I'm worried that some geezers are out to get me,' he said, lighting a cigar.

'Why?' asked Ray.

'Let's just say someone had a word in my ear, and I want you lot to back me up.'

A few minutes later there was a loud knock at the door. Ted went to answer it and returned with Scott, another doorman I knew. He was a mate of both Ted and the blokes at Options. Suddenly, Scott whipped out a sawn-off shotgun from under his long coat and pointed it at us.

'Right. Outside! Now!' he ordered.

Scott was a muppet. What did he think he was up to? There was no way he would pull the trigger. Then, quick as a flash, Ted lunged at him with a knife, stabbing him in the throat. The two of them tumbled to the floor in the hall. Scott was screaming. The next minute, there was an almighty crash and another bloke appeared in the hall brandishing a gun. It was pointing at my head. Everyone ran. I dived behind a wall and slammed the living room door shut. I heard the gun go off. Then came more crashes and thuds. I stood beside the door with my back to the wall, clutching my machete.

After what seemed like an eternity, everything went quiet and I heard the sound of cars screeching away. Gingerly, I emerged from behind the wall. A mate of Ted's was lying on the floor bleeding from the chest and the leg. Ted had blood pouring from his face. Ray and the other guys then appeared from upstairs.

'Bleedin' 'ell, what was all that about?' said Ray.

'Honestly, lads, I had no idea they were coming with shooters,' said Ted.

'Oh yeah,' I replied.

'Look, we'd better get your mate to the hospital,' said Ray.

We took Ted's mate to Kingston Hospital and left him there. We weren't going to hang around in case questions were asked. We then went to The Bishop, a local pub, to review what had happened. Ted told us he knew where the guys lived and wanted to go after them.

'Listen, Ted, I'm not getting into a war over this. It's your problem,' I said firmly. Ray and the others agreed with me.

Knowing that we were already caught up in a war whether we liked it or not, we went immediately to see Bulldog when we got back to east London. After we had explained what had happened, he said he would ring Lenny McLean, who knew Scott. 'Lenny will sort it out,' he said confidently.

Later that day Scott phoned Ray to say that he didn't want a war. Ray told him we didn't want a war either. So we made a peace.

A week later, a masked gang turned up at the nightclub where Ted was working and battered him with hammers, fracturing his skull and putting him in hospital for six weeks. After he came out he wanted revenge, so one night he went to Options and sprayed it with bullets, hitting the manager. He was arrested, convicted and sent down for four and a half years.

Seven

You've killed him

IT WAS 1991, AND I WAS SITTING AT the bar in The Oliver Twist in Leyton having a quiet drink with Steve, the landlord. We were just talking about the end of the Gulf War, when a character named Murphy sidled up to me and whispered over my shoulder, 'When you bump into people you're meant to say sorry.'

'I don't know what you're talking about, mate,' I replied, taking a sip from my pint. I did know what he was talking about, though. I had brushed past him on my way back from the cigarette machine just a few minutes earlier. Murphy was a tall, skinny Irish guy with long brown greasy hair, who for some reason always reminded me of a zip. He was a petty thief, known for nicking cars, and a small-time drug dealer. He was one of those guys who wanted to be a face, but he was a nobody. He was all rabbit, especially when he'd had a few drinks.

'Or else you could get hurt,' he added provocatively, moving closer to me. Steve tensed up, sensing trouble.

'What did you say?' I demanded, turning towards him.

'You heard. Or are you deaf as well as ignorant?'

Something inside me snapped. Grabbing Murphy by the throat with one hand and pushing my other hand into his face, I screamed, 'Ignorant, am I?'

Gasping, he lashed out at me but missed, and the two of us tumbled onto the top of the bar, sending ash trays and glasses crashing to the floor. I struggled with him, then pinned him down and began pounding his head with my fist. I noticed that my shirt was soaked in blood. Murphy had stabbed me.

Then I felt a tingling down my back. Spinning round, I saw Walsh, a mate of Murphy's, waving a Stanley knife at me.

With rage surging through me, I picked up a glass from the bar and smashed it into the side of Murphy's head. He howled like a cat and rolled up into a ball on the floor. His mate started backing away. I hadn't broken the glass first, so it had cut Murphy's head only slightly – but my hand was streaming with blood where the glass had slashed it.

The two of them then fled from the pub, Murphy clutching his head, leaving me dazed and holding my stomach. Peggy, the landlord's wife, told me to get upstairs quickly. She sat me down at a table and cut small strips of plaster to place over the cuts on my hand and stomach and the one across my back.

'John, you should get down to the hospital,' she urged with concern.

'No way. I'm going after that Murphy. He's not gonna know what hit him.' I was seething.

Having found out where both Murphy and the other geezer lived from Steve, I phoned Phil on my mobile. 'Come around straight away! I've some business to finish. And bring a gun.'

I had never shot anyone before, but my hatred for Murphy was so great that I wanted to hurt him badly. The easiest and quickest way to do that was to shoot him. I hadn't decided whether I was going to maim him or take him out completely. No one argues with a man holding a gun. You might be the best boxer, a karate expert, or even someone in the SAS, but when you're looking down the barrel of a gun, you're nobody. It has been said that you should only do the crime if you're prepared to do the time. The way I felt about Murphy, I wasn't thinking of what the consequences might be. The thought of being sent down never entered my head.

Phil arrived at the pub within a few minutes. He handed me a .38 handgun, the same kind as his own, which I slipped into the side pocket of my leather jacket. Then we drove round to the tower block where Murphy lived and went up to his flat on the seventh floor. I didn't bother knocking. I just kicked the door in and we burst through. Sitting terrified in the living room were Murphy's wife and three children.

'Right, where is he?' I yelled, pointing the gun at her, while Phil checked the rooms.

'I don't know!' shrieked his wife, clutching the three kids. 'I haven't seen him since this morning. Leave us alone!'

'Well, when you see him, tell him he's dead!' I bellowed, waving the gun in the air. As I left, I kicked the door with such force that I split the wood down the middle.

Phil and I decided to wait for Murphy in the car. After about three hours, we gave up. He obviously knew I was out to get him, and he was staying well clear of his home. I knew that Murphy sometimes worked behind the bar at a pub called The Beaumont, however, so Phil and I decided to pay him a visit there the next day.

Although it was a sunny morning, my mood was dark as the two of us made our way to the pub. Murphy was about to be taught a lesson he would never forget. We paused for a moment outside the pub, nodded silently to each other, and then pushed the door open.

Apart from a few elderly blokes sipping their pints and reading the paper, the pub was empty. I scanned the bar for Murphy, but could only see an older, bearded geezer whom I took to be the landlord. Perhaps Murphy was in the back or was on his way in.

''Ere, mate, can I 'ave a word?' called Phil when we reached the bar.

'Yes, sir, what can I get you?' said the landlord cheerily.

'Have you got a tea towel?' asked Phil.

'A tea towel?' he said with a puzzled expression. 'But what would you like to drink?'

'Don't worry about the drink. Just get me a tea towel,' growled Phil.

The landlord pulled a face, reached under the bar and handed Phil a tea towel. Then his face went white when Phil put the gun on top of the bar. The barrel was pointing at him and Phil had wrapped his finger round the trigger.

'Cheers,' said Phil, casually covering the gun with the tea towel. 'Now, Murphy. Where is he?'

'He phoned up this morning and jacked in his job,' said the landlord nervously.

'Well, I'm going to leave you a phone number,' said Phil, taking out a pen and scribbling on a beer mat. 'If you hear one sound, you ring that number. Got it?'

'Sure, sure,' said the landlord, putting the beer mat in his trouser pocket. 'I promise you I will. I don't want any trouble.'

When we got outside the pub I suggested that we went to see Pep, a local dope dealer who had his ears to the ground. He did most of his deals in various pubs around the area.

As I expected, Pep was holed up in a local pub, sitting at a table near the jukebox, deep in conversation with a kid in a baseball cap.

'Okay, Pep?' I said.

He smiled and ushered the kid away. 'Hi, John, got some gear for me, have you?'

'Not today. I've some more serious business to sort out. Murphy. Where is he?'

'He came to see me last night and mentioned that he'd cut someone up. When he told me it was Bulldog's son, I knew it was you. I told him he was well out of your league and he should run.' A lot of people thought I was Bulldog's son. I didn't mind. In fact, I felt proud, such was the respect I had for Bulldog.

My anger rose when I heard Pep had told Murphy to scarper, though. 'What are you telling him he should run for?' I demanded.

'What do you mean?'

'I'm looking for this geezer, and you're telling him to run. That's what I mean.'

'I didn't think.'

'Course you didn't think. You never think,' I said, leaning

over the table and jabbing Pep in the chest with my finger. 'Well, you have seriously annoyed me.'

'John. Hang on a minute. I didn't.'

'Stay out of my face, Pep. Do you hear?'

With that, Phil and I left. I knew Pep was scared. It served him right for siding with Murphy, I thought. But I wasn't really concerned with Pep. It was Murphy I wanted. I knew it would only be a matter of time. I would wait for as long as it took – and with Pep telling him to run, it might well be a long time before he came out of hiding.

I continued my search for Murphy, popping regularly into The Beaumont and other pubs where he was known to drink, and generally putting the word about on the street. No one had seen him, though, or if they had, they weren't saying. The fact that within three days of the fight Bulldog had arranged for someone to give a beating to Walsh in the middle of Canning Town one afternoon only made me more determined to track Murphy down.

Around this time, I got married – for money. Through Max, a guy I worked with at Driver's , I had met a Brazilian waitress called Patricia. When she offered me three thousand pounds to marry her and then accompany her to an immigration interview, so that she could apply for British nationality and remain in London to study music and dance, I readily agreed. It sounded like easy money. This business arrangement ended up with us sleeping together. It was great taking her to pubs, as she was a very attractive woman and looked good on my arm. I took her to my dad's one evening. Afterwards he quipped, 'She's got the longest legs I've ever seen!'

Standing there in the room at Walthamstow Registry Office, I was all fingers and thumbs. I felt incredibly nervous. The only people present were a friend of Patricia's, and Max and Bulldog – who had come for a laugh. Patricia, who seemed quite happy, gave Max a camera to record the event.

'You don't want these pictures coming out, John, as they could be used as evidence,' said Max quietly to me.

Seeing how nervous I was, Bulldog whispered, 'You know this is all pretence, son. It's not for real.' I chuckled and began to relax.

A puzzled expression came over the face of the registrar as Max began taking photos of our waists and feet. He couldn't work out what was going on. Bulldog was fighting back the laugher, and my nervousness returned. At the end of the ceremony Bulldog planted a huge kiss on Patricia's lips and grinned. 'This is the only reason I came,' he said.

I was relieved when this debacle was over. Outside, Patricia slipped me an envelope with half my money in it. A few weeks later, after I had filled in the form for immigration, she gave me the rest. A year later she asked for a divorce, because she had met another English guy and had fallen in love with him. I made her give me another thousand pounds for signing all the divorce papers.

Whereas at one time I never went out looking for trouble, I now found myself regularly getting into a ruck with someone. Once I was returning to my stool at the bar of The Beaumont after playing the fruit machine, when a big bloke with tattoos all down his arms yanked the stool towards him and plonked himself on it.

'Excuse me, mate, that's my bar stool,' I said angrily.

'Oh, is your name written on it, then?' he replied sarcastically.

'Yes, it is,' I retorted, giving him a menacing look.

He shrugged his shoulders, got up off the stool, and walked away towards the end of the bar.

It occurred to me that my reputation was on the line. This geezer had just insulted me and I'd let him walk away. I crossed to where he was sitting.

'What's all this "is my name on the stool" stuff?'

'I don't know what you're on about,' he began.

Before he could say anything else, I smacked him full in the face, then again, and again. My heart was pounding. I imagined he was Murphy. Eventually, with blood pouring out of his mouth and nose, the bloke staggered out of the pub and into the street.

One night I was with Bulldog in Kitson's nightclub in Lime-house, which was owned by Terry Marsh (not the boxer). Terry liked Bulldog and me because we never caused any trouble and would help him out at any time. I was sitting at the bar, waiting for Bulldog to return from the gents. As he was coming back, I saw this kid bump into him and spill his drink. The two of them stood there facing each other.

I wasn't having that. I walked over and, with one punch, put the kid on his back. The next minute six of his mates jumped me. I felt a blow on the back of my head. One of them had hit me with a bottle, but it hadn't broken. I went ballistic and lashed out any way I could. One of the bouncers joined me, and between us we threw the kids out.

Back at the bar, Bulldog said coolly to me, 'What was all that about, then?'

'What do you mean? The kid spilled drink down you.'

Bulldog put his hand to his forehead and sighed. 'But John, he was offering to buy me a drink.'

'You what?'

'Listen to me,' he said calmly. 'You need to sort yourself out, boy, because you're going to become everything you don't like in other people. If I go out with you for a drink, I don't want the night to end up in a fight. It's not enjoyable. Take my advice, John, and sort yourself out – before it's too late.'

We left Kitson's and drove to another East End club. Both Bulldog and I liked to move around a bit, as it was a good way of keeping in touch with what was happening in the manor. We were driving through Forest Gate when I acciden-tally rammed the car in front of me at a set of traffic lights. Even though it was my fault, I leapt out and began swearing at the other driver, who had got out of his car to inspect the damage. Then I began laying into him, leaving him slumped across the bonnet.

'John! For God's sake. What was I just saying to you in Kitson's?' said Bulldog when I got back into the car. 'Sort yourself out. You're going to get nicked.'

I wasn't worried about being nicked. Amongst a certain type of criminal there is a feeling of being invincible. You reach a point when you don't even think of being nicked or serving a prison sentence. And even if you were to be caught, you feel you could buy your way out by using a bent solicitor. That was me at that time. I felt invincible.

Then it happened. Someone told me that Murphy often picked his son up from school. I waited outside the school one afternoon, but there was no sign of him. I came back the next couple of days, but again he was nowhere to be seen. Then, a few days later, I was driving past the school when, to my joy, I saw Murphy coming out of the gates with his son. An uncontrollable rage welled up inside me. I jumped out of the car, leaving the door wide open, and marched towards him. He hadn't spotted me.

'Murphy!'

He swung round, and a look of horror appeared on his face. 'Don't kill me!' he pleaded.

'Unfinished business,' I said, advancing towards him. 'Do you remember me?'

Before he had time to reply, I drove my fist into his face, knocking him spinning onto the ground. I put my knee across his throat and began to pummel his head mercilessly. My anger was uncontrollable. I grabbed his ears and began to bang his head on the pavement, oblivious to the screams of the parents and children who were watching.

'You're murdering him!' cried a voice.

When I heard those words, my rage subsided and I got up. I stood there panting, looking down at Murphy, who was lying in the middle of the road, his face and head pouring with blood. 'The next time I see you I really am going to kill you,' I said, turning away and landing one final kick in his ribs.

As I drove away, however, I didn't feel the satisfaction I

had anticipated. I had waited so long for my revenge. Hardly a day had gone by when I hadn't thought about what I would do to Murphy when I caught up with him. But now it had happened, I felt strangely empty.

That night, on my way to work at Nightingales, I phoned Phil on the mobile and told him I had finally done Murphy.

'About time,' said Phil. 'So how do you feel?'

'Great,' I replied chirpily. 'Especially after looking at the blood coming from his head.' Inside, however, I felt strangely let down. Revenge was not all it was cracked up to be.

Two weeks later, I was sitting in The Beaumont on Friday night celebrating a big drug deal, when in walked Murphy's father and brother. They saw me and came straight over. I stood up, ready for them. The father began ranting at me for beating up his son – but what seemed to annoy him more was that I had done it in front of his grandchild.

The guy might have been sixty-something, but I wasn't going to stand there in a pub full of people and take all this. I swiped a glass off the table and slammed it into his face. It shattered immediately, and he collapsed to the floor. The son then went for me, but before he could do anything I whipped out my wasp stiletto, a long, thin knife, and advanced towards him. He backed away, raising his hands. I lunged at him and slashed his arm. The pub went deathly quiet. I could feel everyone's eyes fixed on me.

'Well, come on, then. Do you want some as well?' I screamed, flashing the blade in the air. 'Come on!'

'Oi, John, come on, that's enough,' said a voice.

'Yeah, John, let's call it a day,' said another.

I stood there, the adrenaline pumping through me. Murphy's brother knelt by his father, who was writhing in agony. I scanned the faces in the pub. They were all staring at me. No one was drinking.

I knew no one was going to have a go at me, though. They didn't have the bottle.

'Shall we go for a walk around the corner?' suggested a voice.

I swung round to see a fat geezer coming towards me. Suddenly conscious that I was outnumbered, I backed out of the pub. I went back to my flat, phoned Syed and Andrew, a big black guy I worked with at Driver's who lived nearby, and asked them to meet me at The Beaumont in half an hour. Then I changed out of my suit and into a tracksuit.

Syed and Andrew met me outside the pub, carrying golf clubs. The three of us walked into The Beaumont and began randomly whacking anything and everyone. People dived behind tables in panic or fled outside. The fat geezer was by the pool table. I walked over to him and swung the golf club. It caught his head and he slumped onto the pool table. I then went over to the bar and smashed all the glasses with the club before picking up a bar stool and hurling it through a window. As the three of us left the pub, I shouted to the landlord, 'If the police are called, I'll be back to kill you.'

That night in bed, I reflected that 1991 hadn't been a great year so far.

Just a few weeks later, I was driving across London in the early hours of the morning, listening to Bulldog telling me I had killed a bloke and asking me if I needed money to get away. My first reaction had been that it served the geezer right. He had started it by trying to come back into Nightingales. Then it suddenly hit me. The bloke I had killed might have had a wife and kids. What had I done? I'd taken someone's life. Panic began to set in. Then I consoled myself with the thought that they wouldn't be able to do me for murder, as no one had seen the knuckle-duster. If I was caught, I would be charged with manslaughter. I'd still get ten years for that, though.

I dropped Bulldog off. 'John,' he said, 'if there's anything you need or anything I can do, let me know.'

'Cheers, Bulldog,' I replied, trying to appear laid back.

When I got to my flat on the Beaumont Estate, I rolled a

joint and sat in the armchair, wondering what I should do. It gradually began to dawn on me that I had never been happy. Here I was at twenty-seven years old, with loads of money, a never-ending supply of women, and a reputation as a hard man that commanded me respect. So why wasn't I happy? What was missing from my life?

I wanted to know what had happened after I had made my getaway from the pub, so I phoned one of the doormen. He told me that the bloke I'd hit had been taken away in an ambulance, unconscious, but alive. When the police arrived and began asking questions about me, they were told I was John Howe, an alias I often used.

An hour later Mick, the head doorman at Nightingales, phoned to tell me that the bloke had regained consciousness and was okay. I had nothing to worry about, he said. I felt relief when I heard this. I wanted to believe it. Mick suggested I take a week off.

During this week, many of the faces of the people I had hurt, and the girls I had slept with, flashed through my mind, especially Murphy and the guy at Nightingales. I wondered if the paranoia I sometimes felt from the drugs was here to stay. All the bad things I'd done kept on cropping up in my mind. I saw myself as I really was, without the camouflage of power, reputation and money. It was as if someone had held up a mirror to me – but it was a mirror that showed the inside, not the outside. I began to feel repulsed at the lifestyle my mates were living, because they reminded me of myself.

One afternoon, I was walking with Gary down Walthamstow High Street, where he worked as a butcher, and we were reminiscing about the time when we used to sell furniture from his van and some of the laughs we'd had with Bulldog. Unlike me, he was straight, and had a wife and kids. I will never forget the look of happiness on his face when he told me about the birth of his son.

'What do you do when life becomes meaningless and all you're reminded of is the bad stuff you've done?' I asked him.

'You can't let the past rule your life,' replied Gary. 'You have to keep going forward and boxing on. You're not a bad person, John. Leave the past with God.'

I felt encouraged by his words and my spirits lifted, but I didn't understand the God bit. I went back to work at Nightingales the following Friday, thinking the incident had blown over. I had only been there an hour or so when the police burst in. There must have been about twenty of them. I was arrested, told I was to be charged with attempted murder, bundled into the back of a police van and taken to Vine Street police station, where I was locked in a cell. As usual after I had been arrested for something, I told the police that I wouldn't eat or drink anything or talk to anyone until I had spoken to my solicitor. When I phoned Sherwin, he said he would send a barrister over immediately.

When the barrister arrived, I explained what had happened. He went to see what the state of play was with the police. It turned out that the police had five witnesses who had seen me punch the bloke. The guy had suffered severe haemorrhaging and a broken jaw, and would be scarred for the rest of his life. I told the barrister that I had punched the man, and that he had hit his head on the floor. The barrister suggested that I would probably be charged with grievous bodily harm without intent.

'What's the maximum for GBH?' I asked.

'Ten years,' replied the barrister. 'My advice is to say nothing. If they want to hold an ID parade, they might keep you in for a couple of days.'

When I was taken into the interview room, I replied 'no comment' to each of the detective's questions. I was charged with GBH and given bail. With a GBH charge hanging over me, there was no way I could work as a doorman. If I hit anyone else and was arrested, I would lose my bail and be sent straight to prison on remand.

When I went to discuss my case with Sherwin, he told me that my defence was that I had pushed the guy. He tried to reassure me that I would get off, but I wasn't convinced. Maybe my luck had finally run out.

Eight

Brought to my knees

ONE AFTERNOON, I DROVE OVER TO a mate's flat in Kilburn to play backgammon, but he wasn't in. As I sat in the car waiting for him, I found myself thinking about that conversation with Gary and what he had said about leaving the past with God. I couldn't get it out of my mind. I was sipping a can of Special Brew and smoking some dope, but then I saw a policeman coming towards me. I flicked the spliff out of the window and put the can under the seat. The policeman asked me to get out of the car and take a breath-alyser test. After I had done this, he told me I was under the limit – just. He suggested that I didn't drink any more, but should go home. Feeling fed up, I took his advice.

Back at my flat, I sat alone and found myself thinking how my life was completely messed up. I felt very depressed and empty. It was about 9 p.m. Then I heard what I can only describe as a voice. It was telling me the worst things I had ever done. It must be the TV, I thought, and flicked to the next channel. The voice was still there. I turned the TV off. What was happening? Was I going mad?

Then something clicked inside me: it was the voice we've all heard, sometimes when we've done something good, sometimes when we've done something bad. It was the voice of God, my conscience. The breath was going out of me. It was as if I was dying, and an incredible fear gripped me. I'm going to hell, I thought. I fell to my knees, and tears began to well up in my eyes. 'Give me another chance!' I cried.

Suddenly, I felt as if someone's hands were on my shoulders and I was being lifted up. An incredible warmth overpowered me and the fear immediately evaporated. At that moment I knew – really *knew*, not just believed – that God was real.

I had an overwhelming desire to leave the flat and share this incredible experience with someone. As I closed the door behind me, I looked at my watch and was amazed to see that it was now 1 a.m. Unbelievably, four hours had passed. Then I did something I had never done before: I prayed. 'God, up to now, all I've done is take from you in my life and now I want to give.' What I can only describe as an awesome feeling of love consumed me. This is the most amazing buzz I've ever experienced, I thought. It couldn't have lasted for more than a minute. Then I knew for the first time in my life that I was loved by God. Up until then, I had always thought I was worthless and it didn't matter whether I lived or died.

I couldn't think who would understand this. Who could I tell? Then it came to me: I could tell my mum. She and my stepdad were the only people I knew who believed in God. So I set off for her house, which was about half an hour away. Mum was used to me turning up at all hours, usually drunk and carrying a bunch of flowers.

When she opened the door, I blurted, 'Mum, I think I've found God.'

'What, at 1.30 in the morning?' she replied, rubbing the sleep from her eyes. Alan was standing behind her in his dressing gown.

Mum went into the kitchen to put the kettle on and I sat down in the living room with a puzzled-looking Alan. She came back in, sat on the settee and said, 'Have you been drinking?'

'No, Mum,' I replied. 'Something very strange has happened to me.' I went on to recount that night's extraordinary events. I could see from their faces that they weren't as astonished as I thought they would be. Then I remembered them telling me on a number of occasions how many times God had helped them both in their lives. I also remembered how I had laughed and said that God was just a fairy tale to keep people behaving themselves. Now here I was, knowing that God was real and, what's more, that he loved me.

After I had finished, Mum and Alan both had tears of joy in their eyes. Alan said, 'This is wonderful. An answer to our prayers.'

'John,' said Mum slowly, 'I have something to tell you.'

'What?'

'I've prayed for you every day of your life. But two weeks ago, I felt my prayers weren't being answered. I prayed to Jesus to take you. If it meant you dying, then to let you die, but not to let you hurt yourself or anyone else any more.' She also said she had prayed a nine-day novena to St Jude, the patron saint of hopeless causes.

I knew how much my mum loved me and I knew that, for her to have prayed that prayer, she must have seen the monster I was becoming. I was blown away by the thought that she had prayed for me every day of my life, and I leaned over to hug her. I felt a strong love for her, which I hadn't felt for a long time. It was as though I was seeing my mum in a different light.

Then Alan said to me, 'I've got something for you that belonged to my dad.' He handed me a New Testament. It was the King James Version, he said, and the words of Jesus were printed in red. Then he suggested we say a prayer together to thank God for what he had done in my life. It felt strange, as it was the first time I had prayed with anyone else since primary school.

Lying on Mum's settee that night, I found it very difficult to sleep. I was thinking how exciting life could be, but I also felt fear about how much my lifestyle needed to change. Did I have the strength to do it?

The following morning at breakfast, a voice inside my head kept on telling me that I had imagined the whole thing and that maybe God wasn't real. But I knew he was. I spoke to Alan about it and he told me that the devil is real, just as God is real. 'The devil doesn't want you to know God.

But you know in your heart that what happened last night was where you met God. Don't think too much. Let your heart think for you.' When he suggested I went to see the parish priest, Father Denis Hall, I agreed and asked him to make an appointment.

Later that morning, I made my way to St Joseph's Church, feeling nervous. As I rang the bell, I thought about my last visit there, when my brother David's first child had been baptised. I felt quite different now. Father Hall, a tall, balding man, opened the door with a smile and led me into his living room. Alan had told me that he was a West Ham fan, so I joked that he had good taste. Then I told him what had happened. He listened, then said that it sounded as if I'd had a dramatic conversion, like St Paul, and that I wasn't a nut. 'Trust that what you have experienced is truly God,' he said reassuringly. 'You're not the only one. I've met a number of people who have had similar experiences.' He suggested I went to a place called Aylesford Priory in Kent for a five-day retreat. Even though I didn't know what a retreat was, I agreed to go.

That night, back at my flat, I lay down on the bed and opened the New Testament that Alan had given me. The first story I read was about the prodigal son, who squandered his life and then was welcomed back with open arms by his father. As I read the words, I began to cry. That story was about me. I am the prodigal son, I thought to myself. I'd turned away from God and lived a life of self-gratification with no thought for tomorrow.

A few days later I arrived at Aylesford Priory, set in beautiful grounds on the banks of the River Medway. I discovered it was run by the Carmelites. I was given a room and told the times of the meals – but I still didn't know what I was supposed to do with my time there. That evening, sitting in the library, I took out some dope. I offered it to the two other guys there, but they politely refused.

'Why not?' I asked the older one.

'Because I used to be a heroin addict, and I lost my wife, my kids, my job, everything. I really hit rock bottom and ended up living in a squat, where I wore the same clothes day in day out. I used to lie in my own urine. One day, I remembered what my mother always used to say to me: never forget to thank God. But I didn't think I had anything to thank God for. Then I went to the toilet and as I sat there I thought, I can thank God for this. And as I said it, I felt the Holy Spirit. Eventually I got my life back together. I was reunited with my wife and kids and now I'm a social worker. Now that God's in my life, I realise that I don't need drugs. I just need him. He wants me to be myself, and all that stuff takes me away from being myself.'

Part of me wanted to laugh at the story about the toilet, but I didn't because I could see in the guy's eyes that he was talking about something very real and profound. During my stay at Aylesford we talked a lot, usually sitting by the duck pond. I didn't reveal everything about myself – certainly not the serious villainy or the incident at Nightingales – but we got on well and he could understand where I was coming from.

I felt a great peace during those days at Aylesford, but I didn't speak to any of the priests until the last day, when Father Wilfred McGreal came up to me and asked if I wanted to have a chat. I said yes, and we went to his room. He asked me about my past, but again, I skimmed over it. I just told him I had bought nicked gear and sold blank MOT certificates. At the end of the chat, he told me he was going to give me absolution, which meant that Jesus forgave me. I didn't really understand what he was talking about, however.

Once I'd returned to Leyton, I didn't know what I wanted to do. I was sure of one thing, though: I wasn't going back to being a doorman and dealing drugs. That way of life was leading nowhere other than destruction. Feeling a desire to help others, I started to give some of my clothes and money to various charities and to St Joseph's Church. I got a job as a labourer with Simon's father-in-law. The work was hard, and by the end of the first week I was so shattered that I often fell asleep in my work clothes. Yet I felt that what I was doing was, for once, honest.

By now, I was reading the Bible and praying every day, but I didn't have a personal relationship with God. I saw him as a bit like a headmaster, and I was frightened of him. My prayers consisted of questions, to which I expected answers. One night I was going to put a porno video on, but I suddenly felt it wasn't right. Opening my Bible, I came across the words, 'Get this idolatry away from me.' Straight away, I put all the porno videos in a carrier bag, went out onto the landing and dumped them down the rubbish chute.

I also had real problems with the Catholic Church. I found Mass boring, with all its standing up and sitting down, and I couldn't understand why the Church wouldn't allow divorced people to remarry. The pope just seemed to act like a king, and I couldn't reconcile the idea that the Vatican had so much wealth with the fact that so many people in the world were living in poverty.

I started to pull away from Bulldog, Ray, Phil, Syed and the others. They thought this was because I had been charged with GBH, but I knew that if I carried on associating with them, I would slide back into my old ways. I was still smoking dope, though.

Changing my lifestyle and attitudes was not easy. A lot of my aggression still remained. Just before Christmas, I was backing my car out of the car park under the flats on the Cathall Road Estate when a Rastafarian in a Range Rover blocked my exit and refused to move. 'Come on, mate, it's Christmas. Goodwill to all men and that,' I shouted good-naturedly out of the window. But he got out and started waving a baseball bat at me. Well, there was no way I was backing down. Leaping out of my own car, I opened the boot, whipped out my machete and stood there challenging him. He jumped back into the Range Rover and screeched away.

Another time, after an evening at Walthamstow dog track, I was having a meal in an Indian restaurant in Chingford with my dad, Simon, David and my brother-in-law Geoffrey. My dad and Simon began arguing loudly about something or other. My dad then got up to go to the toilet. As he passed two geezers sitting at a nearby table, I heard one of them say, 'Are you going to shut up, you geriatric idiot?' I was furious. When my dad returned, the same bloke told him again to keep his mouth shut.

That was it. I leapt up, grabbed the bloke by the windpipe and put him up against the wall.

'Aagh . . . What are you doing?' he spluttered.

'Say thank you,' I said, tightening my grip.

'Thank . . . you.'

I released my grip.

'What am I thanking you for?' he stammered.

'You're thanking me for not killing you. If you say one more word, I will.'

I walked back to my table and sat down. The two blokes got up and paid their bill. As they reached the door, the one I'd grabbed shouted back at us, 'We're going to get the guns.'

'Well, make them big ones,' I shouted back. I knew it was an idle threat. If someone is really going to get a gun, they just do it. They don't tell you. What I learned from that incident, I think, was how much I loved my dad.

With the arrival of winter, I began to hate the building work. The pay was poor, just two hundred pounds per week, and I was knackered and dirty at the end of each day. If I was working on the other side of London, I would leave the flat at 6 a.m. and not arrive back until 8 p.m. One day, at a site in Putney, I decided to pack it all in and walked off in the middle of my shift.

The next day, Ray phoned me to say he wanted ten bars of chocolate – in other words, ten kilos of dope. I phoned a guy called Don, who said he would deliver the gear. A few days later, I met Don in a pub and he gave me my cut of five thousand pounds.

That night, however, I felt I had betrayed God by making more money from drugs. The next morning I stuffed the money into an envelope and put it through the letterbox of a local charity shop. Shortly after that, I sold my Mercedes, gave up my St John's Wood flat and signed on.

My mum suggested I went to the Walthamstow Volunteer Bureau, which was based above the United Reformed church, to see if I could take on some voluntary work. Within a couple of weeks, I was collecting pensioners in a minibus and taking them to a drop-in centre downstairs at the church. The drop-in was run by Madge and Arthur, a wonderful married couple who had decided to use their retirement to provide lonely older people with somewhere where they could meet and have an inexpensive meal. When the cook left, Madge asked me if I would cook on Wednesdays. I agreed. I loved the work, even though I was penniless most of the time. I felt I had a purpose. I felt I was worth something.

I also got on well with Christine, an American who was spending a year working at the church and helping out at the drop-in. It became clear, however, that our relationship was not to go beyond friendship. One evening, out of the blue, Christine started kissing me passionately. It felt great and I really missed her when she went away for a week's retreat the next day. When she returned, she stunned me by saying, 'I left America to get away from a guy. I don't want another relationship. I just want to be friends.' I felt very hurt, because I had done things the right way with Christine.

Soon after that, I began visiting the housebound. I will never forget Winifred, who was in her eighties and suffering from leukaemia. Apart from the home help, I was practically the only person she saw. She was a very cheerful, well educated and bright woman who never spoke a bad word about anybody. We became great friends. When I discovered she was a Quaker, we began praying together. I sometimes took her out in her wheelchair to Waltham Abbey, somewhere her husband used to take her when he was alive. Her only other outings were to the local hospital for blood tests. Some time later, when her cancer was in its late stages, I phoned her to see how she was feeling. 'You know, John,' she said, 'I'm looking out of this window and I'm thinking how only God could make a tree.' Since then, I've thought of her words when I've felt down, and they have helped me to see how incredible God is.

I began to search for a deeper sense of God. I was starting to get to know Jesus through reading the New Testament. I found Jesus easier to relate to than God the Father, partly because of my relationship with my dad. One day, after a row over something or other with my dad, I drove to Southend-on-Sea for the afternoon. It was very stormy. Standing there on the beach, with the waves breaking around my feet, I said to God, 'If I can't be completely yours, make one of these waves crash over me and let me die.' I was worried about the GBH charge which was still hanging over me. I couldn't face a long stretch in prison.

For some reason, I found myself thinking of Father Brian O'Higgins, whom I had first met when I was in hospital as a teenager. When I returned to Leyton, I found his address in the Catholic Directory and the next day went to see him in Chelmsford. I talked with him about what was happening to me, and he told me I was a closet Christian. 'John,' he said, 'you need to come out.'

A few days later Andrew, who had been with me when I smashed up The Beaumont with golf clubs, asked me if I could get him two thousand ecstasy tablets. He told me he knew someone who was willing to pay ten quid a tab. 'I'll keep my ear to the ground,' I said, having no intention of doing any more drug dealing. As I walked away, I thought to myself that this had been a perfect opportunity to tell him about God – but I had blown it.

Later on that day, I received a phone call from Double

Duster, who asked me if I knew anyone who wanted ecstasy tablets. If they wanted over a thousand, he said, he could get them for a fiver each. I saw this a trap set by the devil and was outraged.

'Look, Duster,' I said, 'I've found Jesus and I'm not interested in doing any more drug deals. And if you've got any sense, you'll change your life and get to know him.'

Duster when silent. Then he said, 'So you won't be needing your contact book any more. I'll give you eight grand for it.'

I banged the phone down. Then I took my contact book out of the drawer and flicked through all the names and phone numbers I had built up over the last few years. As I watched it burn in the ashtray, I felt that part of my life was over for good.

Still feeling outraged, I went for a walk with Masai and then decided to go to Andrew's flat.

'Listen, Andrew, there's something you should know,' I said to him. 'I'm not going to get you those Es.'

'Why?' he asked, looking puzzled. 'What's up?'

'I've found Jesus and I've given my life to God.'

To my surprise, he replied soberly, 'Say a prayer for me, John, that one day I might know God.'

'I will, mate,' I said, really hoping that he would one day turn his back on crime and let God into his life.

I knew that this moment was a changing point in my life, because I was no longer afraid to speak openly about Jesus. From then on, I began telling people about how I had found God, but I didn't try to convert them. When I told Bulldog, he said, 'I'm not surprised, son, because you have changed. This is fine for you, but leave me out of it.' This was the reaction of all the blokes I'd previously knocked around with.

I sometimes used to go out for a drink with Frank, a committed Communist who worked at the drop-in centre. Despite our different views on life, we got on well. Frank was fascinated by the way I had found God after a life of crime and violence, but always said that he didn't believe in God. Then one day he surprised me by saying that he wanted to explore the possibility of God's existence. I suggested he bought a Bible and started to read it.

A few weeks later, Frank was sitting in a park in Hackney, eating a Kentucky Fried Chicken meal, when a guy sat on the bench next to him and asked for some chips. Frank gave him some chips, and also a piece of chicken. Then the guy pulled out a knife and demanded money. Terrified, Frank replied that he didn't have any money, only luncheon vouchers. The guy walked away. When Frank got home, he opened John's gospel and read the line about 'in giving you receive'. He told me that if he hadn't given the chicken as well as the chips, he might have died. Through this incident he knew God was real, he said.

Eventually the day of my court case arrived and I made my way over to Marlborough Street Magistrates' Court. If I was found guilty of GBH, I could go down for ten years. My defence was that I had pushed the geezer. I had found nineteen witnesses to back me up – even though, apart from the doormen, none of them had been there. The police had found five witnesses to say that I had hit the bloke.

Sherwin had told me that we would be going for what he termed old-style committal. This meant that the prosecution would present their evidence, but I would not have to speak. The magistrate would decide if there was sufficient evidence for the case to go to the crown court. If it did go that far, I had decided that I would not lie on oath: I was prepared to plead guilty and not call any of the false witnesses.

As I sat in the dock and looked at the guy I had attacked, I felt not only anxiety about the outcome of the case, but also a deep remorse at my actions. I had caused him to be in hospital for six weeks. Even now, he was wearing a collar round his neck and leaning on a walking stick, to say nothing of the internal scars he must have had.

I listened to the prosecution barrister outline the case, and it was as if he was describing someone else. I didn't feel that I was the same person, now that I had God in my life.

Then my own barrister stood up and asked the guy I had attacked what he remembered about the incident.

'I was drinking with my friends at Nightingales,' he said, 'and then some bloke asked me to leave. All I remember after that is that I woke up in hospital.'

A second witness took the stand and described how he had seen a bouncer hit his mate.

Then the barrister turned back to the guy I had attacked. 'Is the man who hit you sitting in this court?' he asked.

'He looks like him,' the bloke replied, pointing to me in the dock.

'I'm not asking if he looks like him,' responded my barrister. 'I'm asking if you can be one hundred per cent sure that the man you say hit you is in this court.'

The guy hesitated, his eyes darting around the court room. 'No, I can't be sure,' he said in a barely audible voice. At the time of the attack, I'd had a beard and gelled-back hair which looked dark. Since then, I had shaved off my beard and, because I no longer used gel, my hair looked lighter.

Turning to the magistrate, my barrister said, 'Your honour, the case should be dismissed as there is no evidence against my client.'

A five-minute recess was called. Afterwards, the prosecution agreed to drop the case because there wasn't enough evidence. My sense of relief was enormous, but I was still racked by guilt. To this day, I don't know if Phil and Jim had tampered with the witnesses, but I have to say that it's very possible. Whether they had or not, I knew that the real person I had to thank was God, because he didn't want me to spend ten years in prison. He knew how sorry I was.

One afternoon after the court case was over, I popped into St George's Catholic Church in Walthamstow. I picked up a missionary magazine off a table at the back of the church and began reading it. On the back was an appeal for more missionary priests. When I read this, I felt a strong desire to be a priest overseas, where no one knew me. That night, I wrote to the vocations director, Father Michael Kelly. Given the shortage of priests, I assumed I could be in Africa or somewhere, wearing a dog collar, in just a few months.

The following week, Father Michael came to see me at my flat. He asked me about my life, my practice of the faith and my education. I told him that although I was baptised, I hadn't been confirmed. He then talked about confession and explained exactly what it involved.

'But I can't confess to you, Father,' I said, 'because you would hate me if you knew what I'd done.'

'You are confessing to Christ, not to me,' he replied. 'Our hearts are like a window and when you look through the window, you can see the light and the love. But when you cover the window in mud, you can't see the light and the love. Confession is about taking all that mud and putting it at the foot of the cross, and then you will be able to see again.'

I couldn't bring myself to go through with it. I still felt that Father Michael would hate me if he knew what sort of a person I was. He told me he would pray for me, and then suggested I went on a Youth 2000 Pentecost retreat at Bury St Edmunds in Suffolk.

When I explained to Alan that I was finding confession very difficult, he recommended that I go to Westminster Cathedral. The next day I caught the tube to Victoria. But I felt a little scared of going into a box with someone I didn't know and telling them about all the bad things I'd done. As I sat on the tube, the idea of going for a drink with Simon, who was stationed with the Grenadier Guards at Wellington Barracks, began to seem more appealing than going to the cathedral. I prayed silently to God: 'If you really want me to go to confession today, then you're going to have to show me some sign.' When the train reached Westminster, two buskers got on. They launched straight into 'Hello Mrs Robinson'.

When they sang the words 'Jesus loves you more than you will know', I knew God had answered me.

As I walked into the darkness of the cathedral, I was reminded of the awesomeness of God. It was huge. Looking up, I saw a huge cross hanging above the altar. When I saw the mosaics of biblical scenes, I thought to myself that someone must have spent years sticking them together.

Then I caught sight of the confessional boxes on the far side, and fear gripped me. I felt more scared than when I had stood in the dock facing the GBH charge. I sat down on a bench to wait my turn. A nun was in front of me. Why does she need confession? I wondered. Surely she must be very holy.

Then it was my turn to enter the box. I went in, knelt down and said, 'Forgive me, Father, I'm twenty-seven years old and I've never ever been to confession, even though I was baptised a Catholic.'

Through the grille I saw the priest's face light up with a smile. 'Tell Jesus your sins,' he said softly.

As I was telling him the worst things I'd done, including the attacks on Murphy and the bloke at Nightingales, I felt that there was a tangible peace and mercy coming from him.

'What prayers do you know?' he asked when I'd finished.

'The Our Father,' I replied.

'Well, say an Our Father. Welcome home.'

When I came out of the confessional, I felt an indescribable joy. I had only been in there a couple of minutes. I knelt in the Lady Chapel and prayed the Our Father. I said the words slowly, and the meaning really hit me. I understood that God was my father, and I felt like the prodigal son returning to him. Leaving the cathedral, I felt I could have danced around the piazza. I was now really looking forward to the retreat I was going on the next day.

Early the next morning, I was woken up by someone thumping on the door of my flat. I opened it to find nine police officers standing there. I was arrested for non-payment of various fines – for receiving stolen goods, parking tickets and non-payment of motor vehicle tax – and carted off to Leyton nick. The following morning, I was standing in the dock at Walthamstow Magistrates' Court.

'Mr Pridmore,' began the magistrate, 'I can see that you owe £2,700 in unpaid fines. How are you going to pay?' Before I could answer, she added, 'I can see how this has played on your conscience, because in the last ten years you have paid seven pounds.'

'I've found God,' I replied. 'I've given away all my money and I'm doing voluntary work. I can only afford to pay one pound a week.'

'This court is not willing to wait 2,700 weeks,' she replied sternly. 'You are going to prison for thirty days.'

'No, you don't understand. I'm going on a retreat,' I pleaded.

'No, it's you who don't understand, Mr Pridmore; you're going to Pentonville.'

As I sat in the prison van on the way to Pentonville, I asked God why he wanted me to go to prison rather than on the retreat. Whatever the reason, I prayed that he would use me in whatever way he wished.

At Pentonville I found myself placed in a cell with a young gypsy, who was on remand. We got chatting and he told me he'd got into a fight in a pub. When he was arrested, the police discovered that he was also wanted for burglary. He was very depressed, because he had been unable to contact his wife, who lived on a caravan site in Yorkshire and was about to give birth. When he revealed that he was a Catholic, I invited him to pray the rosary with me. He agreed, although he admitted he hadn't been to church in years, adding that he might not remember the words.

The following morning, a screw walked into the cell and told the gypsy he had some good news. His wife had given birth to a girl and was on her way down to see him. The young guy fell to his knees and said he wasn't going to drink any more and was going to give his life to God. I knew then why God had wanted me in Pentonville, not on the retreat.

As soon as I was released from prison, I phoned Father Michael to explain why I hadn't been on the Pentecost retreat. He burst into laughter when I told him I'd been 'detained at Her Majesty's pleasure'. He went on to say that there was another retreat, at Aylesford, in a couple of weeks.

When I arrived at Aylesford a few weeks later, I was amazed to see about two hundred and fifty young people there, many of them camping. What really struck me was the joy they radiated – but I wasn't really into all that hugging!

The first talk I heard was from Father Slavko. It was entitled 'Give Me Your Wounded Heart'. As he spoke, I found my mind focused on the cross behind him. Then I realised how Jesus had died for me. Although I had read the story of Jesus' passion and death, it had never sunk in that he had died for me. I felt Jesus say to me, 'I would go through this all again for you. That's how much I love you.' Emotions welled up inside me, and I began to cry like I had never cried before.

After the talk, I asked Our Lady what Jesus wanted me to do. I felt the words in my heart that I should go to confession. I asked Father Slavko if he would hear my confession. 'Of course,' he smiled, and I sat with him in the orchard for over an hour, telling him all the sins I had committed. I left nothing out. At the end of it, he placed his hands on my head and absolved me. But they weren't his hands. I felt they were the hands of Jesus. I could feel Jesus' blood running down my face and an incredible love going through me.

Mass still seemed boring to me at this point. Then, during the procession of the Blessed Sacrament, I asked someone what was happening. When they told me Jesus was present, I thought they were mad. How could this be Jesus? Afterwards, I asked a guy who had been kneeling down how he could believe he was worshipping Jesus. I didn't understand it. 'I used to think that,' he replied, 'but I asked Jesus to show me. And he did.'

At Mass the next day, I did just this. 'If this really is you, Jesus, then show me,' I prayed. When it came to communion, I found myself automatically kneeling down. When I went back to my place, I experienced an incredible sensation, similar to that night at Cathall Road. It was a feeling a million times better than any joy I had ever experienced. Then I knew that Jesus was real in the Blessed Sacrament. What's more, all my hang-ups about the Catholic Church vanished. I knew it was the Church Christ had commissioned the apostles to found, and it was the Church where Jesus Christ was truly present.

It turned out that Father Slavko had come to Aylesford with several young people who had claimed to see Our Lady in Medjugorje, a village in Bosnia Herzegovina. This sounded a bit far-fetched to me, especially as the visionaries claimed to have seen Our Lady regularly ever since 1981. When I was told that Our Lady was expected to appear to the visionaries that same day, in an upstairs chapel at Aylesford, I joined the crowd who had gathered in the room below. Kneeling there at the back, I prayed to God to show me if the apparitions were really true. Again, I had another amazing experience of the love of God. I felt that I had been reborn.

At the retreat I met a guy called Troy who, like me, had undergone a dramatic encounter with God. He came from Ilford, where he had been a skinhead and heavily into drugs. One day he went into a phone box and found a picture of Jesus there. That led him to start thinking about God and examining the kind of life he was leading. He abandoned his former lifestyle and made a fresh start. Talking to him gave me great encouragement.

I also met the charismatic Father Stan Fortuna, a member of the Franciscan Friars of the Renewal in New York. A former professional musician, Father Stan used rap music to communicate to the young people. When I told him I wanted to be a priest, he replied that he had wanted to be a priest for nine years. 'It's when you become a priest that the real struggles begin,' he remarked.

When I returned to Leyton, I told Father Hall that I wanted to be confirmed, and also that I wanted to give my testimony. A few weeks later I stood up at a meeting of the confirmation candidates, of which I was one, and spoke about how I had found God. People were crying. At the end of the meeting, Father Hall came up to me and asked me to run the youth club.

One night I was in Ilford, looking for St Peter and Paul's Church. I had been told that adoration, the worship of Jesus in the Eucharist, was being held there. I was a bit lost, and when I came across a small building that looked open, I walked in to ask for directions. Sitting at the bar was Troy. I was in a working men's club. Troy laughed when I explained that I was looking for adoration, and he gave me directions to the church, which was just a few streets away. Reflecting on this incident afterwards, I could see that God had used Troy to lead me to adoration.

Although I knew that God had forgiven me for my sins, I found it difficult to forgive myself, so I began to do penances. Occasionally I would walk six or seven miles barefoot, usually ending up at St Peter and Paul's, where adoration was held daily from 7 a.m. to 10 p.m. I often gave up smoking for long periods and would fast for a week, drinking just water and eating nothing. Sometimes, I stayed up long into the night reading the Bible, to deny myself sleep. When I did go to bed, I often slept on the floor. I offered up these penances for the people I had hurt in my life. I never knew if God was asking me to carry out these penances, but I received great healing from doing them. I began to feel that I wanted to commit myself totally to Christ.

Around this time, I joined the Society of St Vincent de Paul (SVP) and began helping out with their work with refugees, most of whom were Rwandan or Kurdish. I delivered furniture and food to them and sometimes looked after their children. Later, after a special SVP Mass at St James's Church in Spanish Place, I found myself chatting to Cardinal Basil Hume.

'It's so good to see young people involved with the SVP,' he said.

I smiled, thinking to myself, what would he say if he knew about my past?

At a Youth 2000 retreat at Woldingham in Surrey, I consecrated my heart to Our Lady and asked God what he wanted to do with my life. At the time, I was working at the drop-in centre and the volunteer bureau, running the parish youth club – where the kids really opened up to me because of my background – and working with the SVP. In addition, I was studying English and Sociology O levels at a local college. I was often working sixteen hours a day. I felt I had to earn salvation through good works.

Jean Vanier once said, 'If you don't look at the monsters within, you can't tame them.' Over the next two weeks, I began to look at the monsters within me. One of my biggest struggles was learning to forgive myself totally for my past sins. I came to feel that through that consecration to Our Lady, I *was* finally learning to forgive myself, and eventually I understood that God's salvation was free and that I didn't need to do all these good works to gain it.

One day an application form arrived for the post of youth worker on a Hackney council estate. It had been sent to me by one of the staff at the local job centre. I had told her I wanted a job in a caring profession. As I sat down to complete the form, I felt the Holy Spirit telling me that this was what God was calling me to do.

Nine

The concrete jungle

MY INTERVIEW FOR THE POST clearly went well, because a few weeks later I turned up at the Kingsmead Estate as the new youth worker. I knew I was in for a tough time. Hackney was a rough area and the estate, with its soulless, grey tower blocks, was reputed to be one of the worst in Europe. However, with the grace of God, I felt up to the challenge.

I was told that for the first two weeks I would be working with the kids aged between six and fourteen. There were a few problems, as you would expect on a council estate like Kingsmead, but I got on well with them.

I was employed by the Kingsmead Trust, but line-managed by Hackney Social Services. Social Services then asked me to help another youth worker, Everton, restart the Concorde, a youth club for the older kids on the estate. Everton was a large black guy who always wore a baggy tracksuit. I felt a bit apprehensive when I heard I was to work with the older kids, as I knew I would have to work out a different strategy to use with them. Despite these anxieties, however, I still felt that the older kids would respond to the same loving and kind approach I had adopted with the younger ones. They might be older, more streetwise and a bit wilder, but at the end of the day, love would win them over. At least, that's what I thought. And if being loving didn't work, then I always had my hard man image to fall back on.

So it was with a mixture of apprehension and confidence that I greeted the kids when they sauntered into the Concorde that Wednesday night. They were how I'd expected:

nonchalant, loud, aggressive, and curious about this big bloke with the beaming smile. I knew from my time as a doorman that first impressions are vital. In other words, start as you mean to go on. It wasn't long before the first hint of trouble began. A group who were playing pool decided it would be more fun to throw the balls at each other. It was crucial that I handled this in the right way if I was to maintain some sort of order.

'Okay, lads. Come on. That's enough,' I shouted above the noise, trying to remain calm. They just ignored me. If anything, they became even rowdier. 'Come on, lads. Leave it out.' They all laughed and carried on. Then another kid began banging away at the piano. He was no Liberace, that was for sure.

That was it. I marched over to the kid at the piano and slammed the lid shut. He yelped. I'd caught his fingers. I wasn't going to apologise – that was the last thing on my mind. I was going to make sure that this lot knew who was boss here. I picked up a pool ball and flung it at the group by the pool table. Luckily for them, they ducked, but one kid only avoided being hit in the head by a matter of inches. The atmosphere became tense. They eyed me warily. They hadn't been expecting this.

These kids didn't scare easily, though. If anything, they would respond to aggression with more aggression. I stood there in the middle of the room, seething, and shouted that if they carried on like that, I was going to chuck them all out. A skinny kid laughed and called back, 'You're a bigger nutter than we are.'

'Yeah, that's right. I am. Now go on, get out! The lot of you!' I ordered. I was ready to swing for them all. They started to leave, kicking the door as they did so and swearing at me.

Sitting in my flat that night, I realised that I'd blown it with the kids. All the stuff about God's love had vanished in a flash and my aggressive nature had returned. I'd resorted to the tactics I'd used as a doorman. What would have happened if I'd hit one of those kids on the head with that pool ball?

And what about the kid whose fingers I'd trapped in the piano? I might have to deal with his old man coming round to the club with a baseball bat – or, worse still, the coppers. My mistake had been to bring myself down to their level. I has lost their respect. If I was going to win it back, I would have to develop a very different approach.

When I reflected more deeply on this incident, I saw that it said more about me than about the kids. I realised that it was all about control. I needed to be in control so that I didn't get hurt. I'd had no control over my mum and dad getting divorced – and I'd got hurt. Even though I had started to forgive them, I knew that one of the reasons why I hadn't been able to love in the way I should was the feeling I had that I was to blame for their divorce. How far had I let God really enter my life? How much of the hard man was still in me? I wasn't such a changed character as I'd thought. What sort of a Christian witness had I given? 'Lord, let your will be done, not mine,' I prayed that night.

All week I was anxious about what was going to happen when the kids came back to the club the following Wednesday. Everton told me not to worry. The kids would just forget about it. But I needed to watch myself, he warned me. If Social Services got wind of what had happened, I'd be sacked instantly.

Despite Everton's words of reassurance, I was worried that some of the kids would be out to get me. Everton had warned me that they were part of a group that was terrorising people on the estate. Some of them were rumoured to carry knives. Sure, I was a big bloke and I could handle myself – but if a group of teenagers set about you with knives, you don't stand much chance.

Wednesday night arrived. As usual, I had been to Mass that day and I had prayed for patience and wisdom in my dealings with the kids. God was going to have to step in here, I thought to myself. More importantly, I was going to have to let him take control. Instead of the dozen kids who had been there the previous week, around sixty turned up. My worst fears had been proved right. Everton still told me not to worry. He'd been a youth worker for most of his working life, and he reckoned he'd seen it all. 'Take it easy, man,' he said. 'We'll work out a way of handling it.'

The kids dispersed into different corners of the room. Some started playing pool or cards, shouting and arguing with each other. Others lounged around smoking, or listening to the music that Everton had put on.

''Ere, you used to be a hard man,' sneered Chas, a burly youth with squinty eyes.

'Yeah, I was a doorman, if that's what you mean,' I said.

He didn't reply, and went back to rejoin his mates in the corner. A couple of years later, I heard that Chas had been sent down after stabbing someone in the market.

''Ere, mate, he's nicked my game of pool!' cried a small kid.

'So what?' I replied, trying to appear unconcerned.

'Well, it's out of order, innit?' he shot back at me. 'It ain't fair.'

'Okay,' I said casually, 'write down what you want to say on that board.' I handed him a marker pen. He looked a bit puzzled, but eventually went over to the board and scribbled 'No bullying' on it.

Another kid moaned that someone had nicked his sweets. I told him to take the pen and write on the board 'No stealing'. Whenever kids came over to Everton and me to complain about something, we told them to write it on the board.

By the end of the session, we had a dozen 'rules' on the board. Everton and I managed to get the attention of most of the kids, and we asked them how they thought we could best enforce these rules. One kid shouted that anyone who broke the rules should be barred. Another took a more drastic approach and called for them to be beaten senseless. As they argued among themselves about the right way, Everton and I smiled at each other. The kids thought they had made up the rules themselves – and their rules were probably a lot stricter than those we adults would have imposed. Importantly, we had made them feel that it was their youth club, not ours. If they saw it as theirs, they were less likely to cause trouble.

To my relief, the evening had passed without major incident. As the kids left, I asked Ritchie, the one whose fingers I'd caught with the piano lid, how he was. He shrugged and said he was all right.

'Sorry, mate,' I said.

He looked taken aback, but muttered, 'It's all right.'

Most of the kids, I soon learned, were from one-parent families. Many of the mothers had been quite young when they became pregnant, and they often viewed the kids as a restriction on their freedom. A lot of the fathers had legged it when the baby was born. The schools were poor and the options facing most kids when they left was either working in a shop or factory for three pounds per hour, or crime. Many chose crime. Like the drugs that were always on offer, it was an escape route from poverty. At least, that's how many of those young kids saw it at the time. In this sort of environment, the kids felt that nobody cared about them. So why should they care about anyone else?

Unlike the younger kids, the older ones didn't always see me as a glamorous figure. Some of them were doing the same sort of stuff I'd done as they tried to establish a reputation for themselves. They couldn't understand why I'd given up all that power, reputation and money. I tried to get it across to them that this wasn't the way to live, but all that motivated some of them was to attain what I had given up.

One evening, a kid told me that he'd heard about a bloke in prison who had found God. When I asked him what he thought about it, he replied, 'He went soft.'

'Well,' I replied, 'I've worked with geezers who are killers. And they don't tell you about the time when they're sitting alone in the cell crying their eyes out because they hate themselves.' I could tell by the look on his face that he was unimpressed by my answer.

After about three months at the youth club, I was beginning to feel that I was getting nowhere. The kids were much more aggressive and difficult than I'd anticipated. Was I the right sort of person for this work? The anger and aggression I thought I'd extinguished was always simmering beneath the surface.

I went to see my spiritual director and explained to him how I was feeling. He listened patiently, as he always did. When I had finished, he smiled and told me I had to look at the youngsters as plant pots. I was scattering good seeds, and no matter how many bad seeds might also be scattered, they couldn't destroy the good seeds. And the good seeds would grow into something beautiful: Jesus. As I was leaving, he said, 'John, never think that you're not doing anything. You might say something to someone that will change his life, but in ten years' time perhaps. And you will never know this until you get to heaven.'

These words of consolation carried me forward and I thought of them often, especially when I was dealing with particularly difficult kids, such as Duane. Duane had a reputation for being one of the toughest kids on the estate. He was tall, well built and knew how to handle himself.

One evening, a younger kid came up to me and complained that Duane had nicked his game at the pool table. I went over to Duane and said, 'Come on, you know it's his go.' I tried to keep the situation light, knowing that Duane wouldn't want to be seen to have his reputation damaged.

Duane looked me in the eyes and swore at me.

'Come on, Duane, let him have his go,' I replied, ignoring the abuse. As I said this, I gently put my arm on his shoulder. He threw it off violently and tried to shove me away. I was a lot bigger than him, however, and I just stood there, blocking him. The other kids had begun to gather round, sensing that something was going to go off. I wanted to thump him, but, recalling that first night, I managed to keep calm. If I hit him, that would be the end of my youth work at Kingsmead. We stood staring at each other, like they do in those Western films. Who was going to back down first?

The other kids went silent. 'Come on, then, what are you going to do?' challenged Duane, tensing himself.

'What are you getting so upset about?' I retorted. From my tone he could tell that I wasn't going to hit him. If he hit me, however, I knew I would have to hit him back to defend myself. Kids like Duane, out to make a reputation, will go in for the kill.

I watched him and waited for his next move. He studied me. Neither of us was giving anything away. It was a battle of minds. Then Duane suddenly turned and stormed off, shaking his head. Part of me felt humiliated. A nineteen-year-old youth had challenged me to a straightener, and I had backed down.

I went outside to have a cigarette and cool off. A few minutes later, Duane walked past me. 'Have you calmed down?' I asked.

He swore at me. To my surprise, one of his mates said, 'Come on, man, talk to him.'

Reluctantly, Duane trudged over to where I was standing. 'Listen,' he said stonily, 'I don't like being touched.'

I was stunned. Standing in front of me was not a cocky teenager who couldn't give a monkey about anyone or anything apart from his reputation as a hard man. Instead, I saw a broken kid who had shared something from deep within himself. He'd only said a few words, but I knew that what he'd said spoke volumes.

'It's all right. I understand,' I said. 'I was rejected when I was a kid.' He didn't say anything. 'I'm sorry,' I added.

He looked at me and said, 'You're all right, man.'

Working with the older kids was never plain sailing. If things were calm, it was only the calm before the storm. I had to be constantly on the alert and constantly analysing my own responses to situations. God was teaching me valuable lessons, and I had to learn to listen to his voice rather than my own. That's never easy. I was also learning that I had to love the kids even when I didn't want to – which was, I have to admit, very often.

Despite their cockiness and aggressive behaviour, I soon learned that these kids at the Concorde wanted two things: rules and forgiveness. That was how you would win their respect. It was important, I knew, to let the kids know that I wasn't going to hold anything against them. I was trying to put into practice Jesus' words of forgiveness. I was someone who had experienced that forgiveness, and I had a duty to pass it on to others.

Even though Everton wouldn't have described himself as a Christian, he had a kind of faith, was genuinely caring and wanted the best for the kids. He also made sure that any drug dealers steered clear of the youth club. He told me one evening that when he was a teenager he had experienced a major turning point. He'd been asked to take part in a robbery on the same day that a youth worker had asked him if he would help at the club he attended. Up until then, he'd never had any involvement in running the club. He'd just gone there as a punter. He knew he had a choice that day. In the end, he opted to help at the youth club. A few years after we'd worked together at the Concorde, I phoned him to see how he was, and he told me with sadness that one of his sons was inside for murder.

A couple of weeks later, I drove Bulldog to Whipps Cross Hospital for an appointment. He was having terrible head-aches. While I was waiting for him, I got chatting to Tina, a gorgeous blonde in a miniskirt and tight top. She told me she was a single mum and agreed to go out with me that night.

When I went to her flat, we ended up in bed almost immedi-ately. I saw her every day for the next week. However, I knew it was just lust between us. We were using each other. I felt very awkward and bad when I went to see my spiritual director for my monthly meeting. I asked him for confession and told him about Tina. He replied, as I knew he would, that I had to stop seeing her. The next night, I went to see Tina, praying for the strength to resist temptation. She was taken aback when I told her that I couldn't see her any more. She made out that it didn't matter, but I could see from her face that she was hurt and felt used.

One night, I was driving away from the youth club when a seventeen-year-old called Joey, who was standing by the entrance, kicked my car. I decided not to stop and confront him, but to speak to him the following week.

He didn't turn up until two weeks later. He looked surprised when I asked him to come outside with me. All the other kids became excited, thinking I was going to do Joey. I took him over to the car and pointed to the dent. 'You did this, Joey. So what are you going to do about it?' I said in my best hard man voice. I could see that he was scared.

'I didn't do it,' he replied automatically.

He could tell from the look on my face that I meant business. He had two options: to hit me or run. He lashed out at me. I blocked the punch and grabbed him round the neck with one hand. He struggled to break free, but I was too strong for him.

'Come on, what are you going to do about it, Joey?' I demanded. 'You know how it works on Kingsmead!' The kids, who by now had gathered around us, clearly thought I was out of control, but I wasn't.

'You know what I should do to you, don't you?' I said, tightening my grip.

'Yeah, yeah,' Joey squealed. Then he burst into tears.

'But I'm not going to,' I said, letting him go. He staggered back in surprise. The kids looked at each other as if to say, 'What's going on?'

'No, I'm not going to do you, Joey, and do you know why?' He shook his head.

'Because I love you, that's why.'

Joey looked hard at me, not knowing what to make of the situation. The words had stunned him. Probably no one had ever told him they loved him. Coming from anyone else, the words may have sounded wimpish, but coming from a bloke who could have knocked him senseless, they carried meaning.

Alongside my work on the Kingsmead Estate, I was still helping to run the youth club in my parish in Leyton. I was also on the steering committee of the tenants' association on my own estate. On the committee with me was David, a scruffy-looking guy with shoulder-length, wavy dark hair who always wore tracksuit bottoms, trainers and odd socks. I discovered that he had been a company director, but, because of depression, had packed it all in to work as a volunteer advice and information worker on the estate. He survived off state benefits. He was totally dedicated to helping people and some days he would sit in the tenants' association office from 9 a.m. until 9 p.m., just listening to people's problems.

I found out he was a Christian. He had given his life to God at the age of ten, just at the age when I was turning away from God. Considering that his mother had been very violent towards him, I felt it was amazing that he had turned to God in such a committed way. We struck up a close friendship and would often pray together. 'I know it's great to get a hug off people, but I can't wait to get a hug off Jesus,' he told me one day when we were travelling back from the University of North London, where we were doing a course in tenant participation.

One night, I walked into a pub in Leyton to play pool. Standing at the bar was one of Murphy's brothers, the one whose arm I had slashed in The Beaumont. As soon as he saw me, he started to make for the door.

I intercepted him and said, 'Can I have a word?' He looked petrified. 'Look,' I said quietly, 'I just want to say that I've found God and that I'm really sorry, from the bottom of my heart, for what I did to you, your brother and your dad. I apologise, even though I know it probably doesn't help.'

'Are you serious?' he exclaimed. He looked completely baffled and also very wary. I think he was expecting me to hit him.

'Yeah, I've found God. Please tell your dad and your brother how sorry I am.'

'Okay.' He nodded awkwardly and left the pub. I think he thought I was a psychiatric case.

I still had plenty of struggles in my personal life. After a hard day at the youth club, I would sometimes come home to my flat and find myself switching on Sky TV and channel hopping. Some of the programmes I allowed myself to watch did my faith no good. I drew spiritual strength and inspiration, of course, from daily Mass at St Francis' Church in Stratford and also from the young Catholics I met at a fortnightly Youth 2000 prayer group in Canning Town. They provided me with encouragement and a feeling that I was not battling alone.

Money was a problem for me, despite the job in Hackney being fairly well paid. As I'd had so much money before God entered my life, I found it difficult to manage my finances and I was soon in debt. When I was living a life of crime, I never had to worry about money.

As time went on, I began to find it frustrating that I had to play down my faith. I had consecrated both youth clubs to Our Lady and, when I was on my own in the office, I would pray for the kids and for the strength and wisdom to do what God wanted me to do.

One day Chris, my line manager, pulled me up for talking about God in the club. He claimed that only a minority of the kids believed in God. I wasn't buying this, so a few nights later I asked all the kids who believed in God to put up their hands. Out of the forty there, only two kept their hands down. I discovered that some of them were Catholic, some Anglican, others Jehovah's Witnesses or Pentecostals, and some were Muslims. When I next saw Chris, I told him that those who

113

believed in God were not a minority, as he'd said, but the majority. Reluctantly, he agreed I could talk about God.

When I spoke to the kids about God, I focused on his life rather than his rules. I knew from my own experience that when you know God loves you, you will want to keep his rules. I tried to encourage them to pray in their own way and not to give up.

Some weekends I used to take the kids to an adventure centre in Sussex. Although I didn't get paid for it, I felt it was vital to get them out of their home environment. Everton would take us down in the minibus on Friday night and collect us on Sunday afternoon. At the centre they could go sailing, canoeing, rock climbing or horse riding. They loved being in the country and seeing all the animals. It was so different from the concrete jungle of Kingsmead. Here they could feel free and release all their energies in a positive way.

As I got more confident in my work, I looked at new ways of getting the kids involved in the estate. Social Services had appointed a community artist, so I got the kids to paint on 4 x 4 boards their images of the estate and what they wanted it to be. These pictures were then displayed around Kingsmead. Most of the kids painted flowers and trees, the opposite to what they saw every day. The organic garden was another success. We cultivated a small piece of land beside the youth club and grew tomatoes, lettuces, onions and rhubarb. The kids then delivered all the produce to the elderly living on the estate.

After two years at Kingsmead, I felt it was time to move on. Although I felt I was doing God's will, there was something missing in my life. I had a strong desire to give up all my possessions and follow Christ totally. That was why I had applied to live in community for a year at the Family House of Prayer, near Dalmally in the Scottish Highlands. I was excited when they agreed to accept me.

I was choked when it came to saying goodbye to the kids at my last session at the Concorde. Looking at them, and knowing the kind of homes many had to go back to, I felt a real tug at my heart strings. But I knew that God wouldn't stop loving them just because I wasn't there.

After we'd cleared up, Everton invited me to go for a drink with him in the pub up the road. I was in good spirits, reflecting on two of the hardest years of my life – two years when I'd learned more from the kids than, perhaps, they had learned from me. I'd tried my best. I'd failed a number of times and more than once had wanted to pack it all in. Yet I'd glimpsed the hand of God at work and, as my spiritual director had told me, I'd been scattering seeds.

Everton and I were sitting in the corner of the pub when a group of youths strolled in. I didn't take much notice of them, but when they came towards us, I realised that one of them was Duane. What did he want?

He halted a few feet from us, not saying anything. I smiled at him. He smiled back uncertainly and then, to my amazement, asked me if I wanted a drink. When he handed me the drink, he thanked me for all that I'd done, before disappearing with his mates to the other end of the bar. That incident said to me that all my work at Kingsmead had been worth it.

Ten

All your sins are weaknesses

I STOPPED MY CAR ON A REMOTE, winding road in the Scottish Highlands and walked down to a waterfall. I sat there taking in the beauty of the mountains. The only sound was the gushing water. I began to pray and reflect on how my life had been changed by God. Here I was, with all my worldly possessions in one black bag. I started crying as I thought about how good – and patient – God had been in bringing me to this point, and I thought about my past life, the kids at Kingsmead and my dog Masai, whom I'd given to David from the tenants' association to look after. I felt liberated and excited by what lay ahead. I no longer had a flat and, when David came up to visit me at the Family House of Prayer, I would no longer have a car.

Situated in Argyllshire, the Family House of Prayer was set in beautiful grounds containing a small pond and exotic plants and skirted by the River Orchy. It was surrounded by forests and mountains. To the west was Beinn Cruachan, which was well over three and a half thousand feet high, and to the east was Beinn Lui, which was around three thousand feet high. The nearest road was a mile away. The Family House of Prayer was really three houses: Craig Lodge, which contained the chapel and dining room, Craeg Meon, where guests stayed, and Craeg Beag, where the community lived.

I found myself with four other people who had also decided to spend a year in community there – Alve, Therese, James and Gez. Gez, who was from Manchester, had been a heroin addict. He told me he'd hated himself so much that he'd bitten lumps out of his arm. His life changed dramatically when he had an experience of the Holy Spirit while sitting in the back of a police van after he'd been arrested for something. As I've discovered, God can reveal himself to us in the most unlikely places and when we least expect it.

Each day began in the chapel with Morning Prayer at 7.30 a.m., followed by breakfast. Between 9.30 a.m. and noon we all did manual jobs in the house or grounds. I often helped to chop wood from the forest. After midday prayer we met for lunch, along with Mary Anne and Calum, who set up the Family House of Prayer in 1988, and Penny and Steve, who managed the house and any outside community members, such as Robert and Jenny, a young couple who lived in a caravan in the grounds. From 2 to 4 p.m. we helped to make items such as icons and rosaries. Then, following an hour of spiritual reading, we met for prayer at 5 p.m. After the evening meal, we met for the rosary and holy hour. By 10 p.m. we were all usually in bed.

Initially, it was difficult to adjust to such a disciplined life. Obedience was one of the hardest things I had to learn. While I enjoyed chopping down trees and working in the grounds, I hated having to clean the toilets. After a few weeks there, however, I slotted into the daily routine.

One of the reasons why I had come to the Family House of Prayer was to see if I had a vocation to the priesthood or religious life. I had felt at Kingsmead that, as much as I enjoyed the work and felt I was doing God's will, there was something missing. When Father Glen Sudano, the vocations director of the Franciscan Friars of the Renewal in New York, came one weekend to give a retreat, I told him this. He suggested that I visit his community in New York after my year in Scotland, to continue my explorations.

I also met Bishop Roddy Wright of Argyll and the Isles on several occasions. Somehow he always seemed a very broken and sad man, and yet I remember him giving one of the greatest homilies I've ever heard about the true presence of Christ in the Eucharist. Not so long after that, he ran away with a woman. It just goes to show how God can use us no matter what our situation.

Living with four other people day in, day out was not easy. There were times when I skipped evening prayer, and some occasions when I came close to quitting the community. One evening I was so fed up with community life that I decided to go to the pub in the village and get smashed. Then I felt God saying to me that the only difference it would make would be that I would have a hangover in the morning. I went into the chapel instead. Another night, I was playing pool in a pub in Dalmally when I got chatting to a woman. She was very flirty and invited me back to her house. It was so tempting, but I prayed for strength and said no.

I had always been curious about Medjugorje, the village in Bosnia where Our Lady had been appearing to some young people since 1981, so I was thrilled to be offered a trip to an international youth festival there with a group of Irish pilgrims. Once there, I felt an amazing peace and had no doubts that Our Lady was present. One day during the trip I went to confession three times. That evening, I found myself once again in one of the confessionals by St James's Church. I'd heard that Father Philip Pavitch had an excellent gift as a confessor.

'I don't understand why I'm here, Father,' I said. 'I've already been to confession three times today.'

'It's the sins of the past,' he replied.

'But I've confessed all my sins of the past,' I said.

'The ones that still bother you, confess them in detail, leaving nothing out.'

I did this. At the end, he said a prayer over me, and I knew that those sins would never bother me again. I now understood why Our Lady had asked me to go to Medjugorje.

Towards the end of the year, I went back to London to ask David for my car back. I needed it to travel around Scotland delivering posters and fliers for a theatre production that a friend was staging. There was no answer when I phoned him, so I went round to his flat. The kitchen light was on, but there was no reply when I knocked. I shouted through the letterbox. After a couple of minutes David opened the door, looking pale, shabbily dressed and unshaven.

'You know, John,' he said, 'I've been suffering from a terrible headache these last few days. But as soon as you shouted my name, it disappeared.'

'How do you fancy coming back up to the Scottish Highlands for a few days?' I asked, thinking that a change of scenery might do him good.

'Great. I've not been feeling well recently. I don't know what it is,' he replied.

The next day, as we drove up to the Family House of Prayer, David told me he wanted to become a Catholic, but added that he had a problem with the honour Catholics paid to Our Lady. This, I think, had something to do with the way his mother had treated him.

He thought the Family House of Prayer was fantastic – and everyone there loved David, because he had the rare gift of being a good listener and he was never judgemental. Some evenings he would go down to the local pub to write his diary. One afternoon, he came into my room after a walk in the hills, looking very emotional.

'John,' he beamed. 'I've found my real mother – Our Lady!'

A few days later, I went to David's room to tell him that there was a special meal downstairs to celebrate my year in the community. I knocked on the door, but there was no answer. I knew that David often had a sleep in the afternoon. When I opened the door, however, I was shocked to see David lying half on his bed and half on the floor, looking very ill. Vomit was everywhere. As I helped him up onto the bed, he murmured, 'Thank you, John. Thank you.'

Alve appeared at the door and I asked her to phone for an ambulance. I sat with David in the back of the ambulance for the journey to the hospital at Oban. Alve asked a priest to come to the hospital to baptise David. We knew it was what he would have wanted. After examining him, the doctors decided he needed specialist care, so they transferred him to Glasgow Central Hospital. Very worried, James and I followed the ambulance in my car. David was critically ill, so the ambulance travelled very slowly.

I stayed with David for three days, holding his hand and praying. His mother and sisters arrived. I found it difficult to know what to say to his mum, as I knew how badly she had treated him when he was young.

On the third day, David was pronounced dead. A doctor told me he had died of a brain haemorrhage. With tears in my eyes, I punched him playfully in the chest and said, 'You're up there now, mate, so look after me. I've got to carry on down here.'

As I left the hospital, I felt angry with God and burst into tears. Why had he allowed David to die? He was only thirty-eight. Apart from priests in the confessional, David had been the only person I could talk to about absolutely anything. Why had this happened?

When I arrived back at the Family House of Prayer, I was asked if I would sort through David's belongings. I found a letter addressed to me. In it, he wrote that he could understand it wasn't his fault that his parents couldn't love him in the way they should have done. He went on to thank me for my friendship. It was as if he had known he was going to die and he was saying goodbye. I also found his diary. Reading it, I discovered that what he had been writing in it each day was, in fact, a letter to God the Father.

I decided I needed to be on my own for a while to come to terms with David's death and my feelings towards God, so I went to the island of Iona. Sitting in the abbey there, I found myself staring at a small icon of Our Lady and the infant Jesus. I felt that the baby was David. As I lit a candle in front of the icon, I felt that Our Lady was standing on one side of me and David on the other and they were hugging me. When I came out of the abbey, I was no longer angry with God.

Instead, I thanked him for the gift of David. The impact that David had on the lives of those on the Cathall Road Estate was obvious from the fact that around six hundred people turned up at his funeral in Leytonstone.

Just before I left the Family House of Prayer, Mary Anne asked me what I had learned about community. I thought for a moment and then said, 'I feel that I'm leaving with a good relationship with all the other members, and that I understand the importance of obedience in community life. And I realise now that the key to peace is prayer. If you don't put aside time to pray each day, then you will never have peace.'

She grinned and said, 'This is why we set up the community, for people who have changed like I've seen you change.'

A couple of weeks later, I flew out to New York to visit the Franciscan Friars. A wealthy visitor to the Family House of Prayer, who had been moved by my testimony, had given me the air fare. I spent two months living and working with the community, at their houses in the North Bronx and the South Bronx, learning about their work with the poor. I was impressed by their simple and prayerful life, and felt that this was where God was calling me, so I made up my mind to join the community.

Then I returned to the Family House of Prayer for two months to help out with the summer retreats, before heading back down to London. I hadn't been back long when I received a phone call to say that Bulldog had died of brain cancer. He had, I knew, been ill for some time. The last time I'd met him, I'd given him a Divine Mercy card. When he read that God would not turn away the worst sinner in the world, he replied with a smile, 'Well, I've got nothing to worry about then, have I?'

Bulldog's son Ray asked me to give the eulogy at his funeral, which was to be held at an Anglican church in Chingford. The funeral was a big affair, with many top villains present. Many of the blokes I knew hadn't seen me since the time I hit the guy at Nightingales. As I walked into the church,

I felt very nervous and prayed to God to direct me in what I said.

When it came to the eulogy, I slowly made my way to the front of the church, took a deep breath and said a prayer to the Holy Spirit. Bulldog's wife Peggy was sitting with Ray in the front row. I began to talk about my conversion, then spoke of how, in the last few months, Bulldog and Peggy had begun to pray each night. By the time I'd finished, some of those in the church, including a couple of faces, were crying.

As we were leaving the church and making our way to the cemetery across the road – the cemetery where the Krays are buried – one of Bulldog's nephews ridiculed me and accused me of telling lies about Bulldog praying. Peggy overheard this and reacted angrily. 'It's true,' she said. 'He did, with me. And you should have more respect.'

We all went to a pub in Leyton afterwards, one of Bulldog's favourite haunts. Part of me hadn't wanted to go to the wake, but when I asked myself where Christ would be, I knew I had to go. A number of geezers came up to me to ask about how I'd found God. I told them that God could change their lives, just as he had changed mine. They listened intently but, I suspect, sceptically.

In August, accompanied by Gez from the Family House of Prayer, I drove to Walsingham for the New Dawn Conference, the largest gathering of Catholic charismatics in Britain. It was a great retreat. I remember meeting a fifteen-year-old girl one afternoon when I was having a ciggy outside one of the tents. As we chatted, she revealed that she enjoyed listening to Def Metal music. She was taken aback when I told her that when she went home she should smash up her CDs, as this music was influenced by Satan. Two years later, I met her at another retreat and she told me she'd done what I'd said and her life had been transformed by Jesus.

'I think I'm going mad!' she beamed.

'Why?' I asked.

'Because I can't stop talking about Jesus,' she replied.

'You're not going mad,' I told her, 'you're falling in love.'

Another youngster who had a life-changing experience was Declan. He'd been expelled from four different schools and was only at the retreat because his parents had made him go.

'You don't believe in God, do you?' I said.

'No, it's a joke,' he replied crossly. 'My parents make me go to Mass and pray the rosary, but it's all rubbish.'

'Well, go home and ask God if he's real,' I said.

Two weeks later, Declan phoned me to ask if I would take him on a retreat.

'No,' I said. 'I'm not taking you on a retreat just because your parents want you to go.'

'But I want to go. I went home and asked God if he was real, and he showed me that he loved me.'

Today, Declan is a member of the Youth 2000 mission team and spends his time giving retreats in Catholic schools.

A few days after New Dawn, along with James and Alve and about thirty young Scottish Catholics, I travelled to Paris for World Youth Day. I'll never forget standing on a race course with a million and a half joyful young people listening to Pope John Paul speak with such belief in and love for Christ. At one time the pope had seemed an anachronism to me, but in Paris I understood that he really is the successor to St Peter.

The spiritual boost I'd received in Paris soon disappeared when I returned to my flat in Cathall Road. I hadn't seen any TV since going to the Family House of Prayer, so that night I began to channel surf and ended up watching porno movies on Sky TV. When I went to bed, I masturbated for the first time in eighteen months. In the morning, I felt downcast, ashamed and in need of God's forgiveness. I set off early for Mass, in order to catch the priest for confession.

Afterwards, I knelt in prayer in the church. It turned out that a number of children were making their first holy communion that morning. As I looked at the girls in their white dresses and the boys in their suits, my spirit lifted and I felt

God was saying to me, 'I love you.' I realised that it was only through the grace of God, not my own willpower, that I hadn't masturbated for so long. Masturbation is a subject that is rarely openly discussed in the spiritual life. It is, however, something that many Christians struggle with and many are too ashamed to talk about. I remember a priest once explaining that masturbation happens when you allow a lustful thought to grow in your head. That thought soon turns to fantasy, and the fantasy turns to action. In order to avoid masturbation, you need to stop at the thought. We're all tempted. And Jesus was tempted, of course. In order to reduce the temptation, I phoned Sky TV the next day and cancelled my subscription.

I didn't know what I was going to do in the year before I joined the Friars. I was also having money worries, largely from the debts I had built up during my time at Kingsmead, so I signed on again. Although I had paid off around a thousand pounds of my debt, I still owed one and a half thousand. I prayed about it, but there didn't seem to be a way out. I was well and truly on my uppers.

A few days later I got a phone call out of the blue from Ron, the chairman of the youth club at Kingsmead. He asked me if I would be interested in working there for a month to set up a car mechanic project. I had put in an application to the National Lottery to fund the project while I was working at Kingsmead. They had now decided to give a grant of sixty-two thousand pounds to start it up. For the month's work, Ron added, I would get paid one and a half thousand pounds. I couldn't believe it. He then went on to say that if I wanted to manage the project for a whole year, then I could. My decision to join the Friars in the Bronx meant that this wasn't possible, however.

So I returned to Kingsmead. It was good to see some of the kids I'd worked with before, and they were pleased to see me. The project worked as follows. The youth club would receive cars that had been impounded by the police, and a mechanic would teach the kids basic maintenance, such as changing spark plugs, points, etc. They would then be put through their driving test by the British School of Motoring (BSM). After they'd passed their test, they would be allowed to drive fully insured cars from a car pool, free of charge. They would be allowed to take a car for a couple of days at a time. The idea behind the project was to cut down car theft. If the kids had access to cars, then they wouldn't want to nick them. The reason why most of the kids stole cars was because they hadn't passed their test or they couldn't obtain insurance, especially if they'd already been banned from driving.

Finding a premises, a mechanic and a project manager, and liaising with Sun Alliance insurance and BSM meant that I was very busy for that month. Anyone who has ever set up a project from scratch will know how difficult it is to pull together different organisations and individuals and get them working towards a common aim. I succeeded, however, and left Kingsmead feeling that I'd accomplished something very worthwhile.

One evening, I was having a drink in a pub in Leyton when, at the end of the bar, I saw a familiar face from the old days: Andrew. He spotted me also, and came over.

'John, you've been praying for me, haven't you?' he grinned.

'I have, mate.'

'Well, I'm now married with kids, I've got a nine-to-five job, and I'm close to the Lord.'

I laughed and gave him a hug. 'Praise God, mate.' Not for the first time, I realised how effective it is to pray for someone.

I was finding it difficult living on my own. I really missed not having a community and the Blessed Sacrament close by. I have to admit that I've always found it very hard to live the Christian life without a good support network. Of course, some people are suited to the solitary life, but living as a hermit has never appealed to me. I think I would go mad.

Then Father Fred de l'Orme, whom I'd met at the Family House of Prayer some months before, phoned me and asked if I would like to become a youth worker in his parish of St Joan of Arc, Highbury, in north London. He explained that he didn't want what he called 'the traditional youth club' – i.e. pool, table tennis and discos – because he felt this didn't bring the kids any closer to God. Instead, he wanted youth activities that had a stronger spiritual element. Delighted by his offer, I accepted the post immediately and arranged to move in the following week.

The parish of St Joan of Arc is situated between Finsbury Park and Islington, and when I was there it had a Sunday Mass attendance of around six hundred. It was a fairly typical inner London parish, containing a mixture of working-class and middle-class parishioners, and a significant number of people from other countries. Father Fred provided me with food, a room and travel expenses, and I signed on each week so that I would have money for essentials – as well as a packet of ciggies.

I found myself working alongside Karen, a twenty-one-year-old with long, straight brown hair, almost olive skin and a beauty spot on her left cheek. We set up a confirmation programme of seventeen two-hour sessions. Each session concluded with half an hour's adoration of the Blessed Sacrament. Father Fred supported our idea and agreed that it was crucial to give the teenagers some solid spiritual nourishment, as this would be the last chance to do so before they left school.

Forty-six youngsters, aged fourteen and fifteen, signed up for the programme, the largest number in the parish for a long time. But when the parents – many of whom never went to Mass – heard of our plan, some of them were unhappy. They felt it was too heavy.

On the opening night, we told the kids that they were only allowed to miss two classes, unless there was a good reason for their absence. It soon became apparent to us that, because of their attendance levels and attitude, some of the kids were not ready to be confirmed. When I told Father Fred this, he said he would explain the situation to them and their parents.

He phoned the parents and asked them to come and see him the following week to discuss their child's confirmation. But then he went away for a week, leaving Karen and me in charge of the presbytery.

One evening, some of the parents turned up, demanding to know why their children weren't going to be confirmed. I took them into the living room and tried to explain the reasons to them. Watching their reactions, I could tell that this was not going to be a smooth meeting.

One man began swearing at me. 'I'll tell you something, mate, if you don't allow my kid to be confirmed, then I'll do you!'

For a split second, I wanted to thump him. Instead, I smashed my hand on the table and the room suddenly went silent. 'Now, listen to me. I give up my time for your kids as a volunteer. And every one of the people involved is a volunteer. If you have a problem with anything we do, then speak to Father Fred, because I don't want to hear it.' Then, turning to the abusive character, I said, 'And if there's one more sound out of you, I'll take you outside and beat you senseless.' He didn't say another word.

Later that night, I felt guilty about my behaviour, even though I'd had no intention of hitting the man. I knew that to threaten someone with violence was not the way of Jesus. I'd felt, however, that the man was trying to intimidate me with his aggression and threats and that he needed to be brought down a peg.

We continued with the programme, and tried to make it as interesting as possible by using guest speakers and putting a lot of thought into reconciliation sessions. Many of the kids went to Mass regularly after their confirmation, even though their parents didn't. We also began a prayer group and a Bible study group.

The parishioners at Highbury were aware of my past, and some of them found it difficult to come to terms with the fact that I was living in the presbytery. As a result there was a lot of friction. At one parish meeting, Father Fred opened the Bible and pointed to all the sinners God had used. 'Look at Moses, a murderer, David, an adulterer, Paul, a persecutor of the Church,' he said. 'God uses anyone he chooses.'

By this time Karen and I were growing very close, and we soon found ourselves kissing regularly. We never allowed our relationship to go any further – although both of us found this difficult. I remembered how hurt I'd been when my relationship with Christine ended, and also how hurt Tina had been when I broke off that relationship. Part of me enjoyed having female company and going to restaurants and cinemas, but, knowing that I was soon to go off to the Friars, another part of me was deeply troubled by the fact that I was falling in love. I knew the relationship had no future. What's more, both of us found it a big struggle to be chaste.

Around this time, I began to make a consecration to Our Lady, based on the writings of St Louis de Montfort. I had read that Pope John Paul had done this and it had changed his life. Soon after I'd finished the consecration, which took thirty-three days, I was invited to meet Robert Toone, national leader of Youth 2000. He asked me if I was willing to be the regional leader for London. This would, he explained, involve organising retreats for young people. At the time, Youth 2000 only ran a few retreats each year.

'No. I'm not the right person, Robert,' I replied, surprised by his offer.

'Why?' he asked.

'Well, I'm very stubborn and I like to get my own way.'

'That's what I need: someone strong who can get things done.'

'And I'm going to join the Franciscan Friars of the Renewal next year,' I added.

'That's fine. Take the job on until you leave.'

I thought for a moment. 'Okay, if you think I can do it,' I said finally, wondering if I was making the right decision.

'But I'll have to ask Father Fred if he'll allow me to combine my parish work with Youth 2000.'

Father Fred felt that I would be good as a regional leader. This gave me a lot of encouragement.

A few weeks later, I was asked to lead a retreat at Maryvale, near Guildford. While I'd helped out at retreats before, I'd never led one, so I was a little apprehensive when I arrived at the centre, along with the two hundred retreatants.

Then I remembered that a year or so before, I'd attended a retreat at Allington Castle in Yorkshire, led by Father John Edwards SJS. He'd come up to me one day and asked if I would pray with him over some people. I felt very privileged but also, as I told him, uneasy, as I was very sinful.

'All your sins are weaknesses,' he said.

Hearing these words lifted my spirits and gave me a renewed sense of purpose. I spent most of the night praying over people. At the end, I knelt down for Father John to pray over me. When I stood up, he said he had some words for me.

'John, you're going to be a great leader and bring thousands of souls to God.'

At the time, I thought this was crazy. I had no experience in ministry at all. How could I bring souls to God, especially with my past?

I also remembered listening to a tape by an American retreat-giver. She said that she talked to thousands of people all over America and that she wanted to be loved and liked by them. This is okay, she said, so long as you give it to Jesus before you speak and ask him to use you in whatever way he wants.

So before I began the retreat at Maryvale, I did just this. I asked Jesus to take all my pride and use it. The retreat went incredibly well. Several people came up to me and said that it sounded as if it was God speaking, not me.

One afternoon Troy, whom I'd first met on retreat at Ayles-ford and who was now Brother Francis and a member of the

Franciscan Friars of the Renewal, came to see me. He was in England to give some talks in various parishes. When he suggested that we ran a free Youth 2000 retreat, I told him that it sounded a great idea, but what about the funding? He said we should hold a weekend retreat in Ilford, where he came from, and it would cost around three hundred pounds. He suggested that everyone could sleep in the parish hall and in one of the classrooms in the school next door.

When I told Robert about the idea he said fine, go ahead, but emphasised that I was responsible for finding the money. What's more, I wanted Father Harold from the Friars to come over for the retreat. He was a brilliant preacher – but his return flight would cost around four hundred pounds.

I decided to put my trust in God and take the plunge, and I began giving talks in local parishes and schools. The average number of people on a Youth 2000 retreat was between forty and fifty. Eighty-five people booked up for the one in Ilford. Several priests, including Father John Armitage from Canning Town, agreed to help out on the retreat.

During the coffee break on the first day a guy called Neil, who was a few years younger than me, came up and told me he had come to the retreat after hearing me give a talk in his parish. He said, 'Everything stopped for me when you said that six years ago you met a man who changed your life. And when you said that man's name was Jesus, it was like an arrow going through my heart and I knew I was going to belong to Jesus for the rest of my life.'

During the retreat Neil went to confession for the first time in twenty years. He had been an altar boy, but during his teens he had fallen away from the practice of his faith. I persuaded him to give his testimony at the end of the weekend. Standing up at the front of the hall, he began to talk about how, after being beaten up at a football match, he'd joined West Ham United's notorious Inter City Firm, a group of violent football supporters. He would travel around the country with the gang, engaging in acts of violence and vandalism. One of the incidents that caused him to leave the group, he revealed, was when he witnessed seven men stab an Arsenal supporter. He had been in plenty of fights, but had never engaged in this sort of violence. After this, he was physically sick and vowed never to go to a football match again.

He also told us how he had worked for an internet company which, he felt, was very satanic. He said he felt he was dying from within through working there. His character changed so much that his mother, a practising Catholic, was worried. She urged him to pray. The only prayer he could remember was the Hail Mary. When he said it, a real peace came over him. He found an old Gideon Bible upstairs, and when he opened it he saw some words he'd written when he was a child. He realised that what he'd lost was his innocence. He prayed, 'God, I want my innocence back.' He then began reading the Bible each day, and three months later he went to Mass for the first time in eighteen years.

Neil's lifestyle, he admitted to me, had been based around drink, drugs and sex, and he had nearly died on several occasions because of it. 'John,' he said, 'I'm scared that when I leave the retreat and go back home, I'll go back to the way I was.'

'Well, don't go back. Join us on the school retreat we're going to do in Manchester.' I said this without thinking. It must have been the Holy Spirit prompting me.

I had also planned a retreat at Worth Abbey in West Sussex. Robert and I had argued about whether or not the retreat should be free. At the end of the Ilford retreat a collection was taken which brought in nearly one thousand pounds, so I felt strongly that we should trust God to provide for us again. Robert said that there was no way it could be free. I told him that only a few people had booked up and there was only a month to go. 'Robert, if we want to get the people for this retreat, then it has to be free.'

In the end, we compromised. First-timers were charged just

ten pounds, and everyone else paid fifty pounds. About four hundred people turned up, two-thirds of them first-timers, and it went fantastically well. At the end, Robert came up to me and said, tongue in cheek, 'Well, thank you brother. You're swanning off to America and I've got a bill of several thousand pounds.' But we found all the money to cover the costs.

After that, I went to spend some time at my mum's, as my stepdad Alan was quite ill. One night, at about 3 a.m., I heard Mum calling me. When I went into the bedroom, I thought my stepdad was already dead. He looked so pale. I knelt down beside him and began praying the Divine Mercy prayer.

'I'm going to call the doctor, John,' said my mum.

'Call the priest first,' I said.

The priest soon arrived and administered the last rites before Alan was taken by ambulance to Whipps Cross Hospital, with us following in my car.

We stayed with him until late morning, then left to go to lunchtime Mass in Stratford. When we returned to the hospital, we were told that Alan had died at 12.16 p.m. The Mass had begun at 12.15, and we had offered it up for him. We had both felt a real sense of the Holy Spirit during the Mass.

At Alan's funeral at St Joseph's the following week, I felt an incredible closeness to him as I was praying, as if he were saying to me, 'I'm happy now I'm with God.' I remembered that it was Alan who had not only given me my first New Testament, but also arranged for me to see Father Hall, the priest who was presiding at his funeral. I realised how much God had used Alan to bring me closer to him. These words came to me: 'Anyone who brings me one soul, his soul is saved.'

That year I learned to trust God more and more. In November I'd felt God was saying to me that I should sign off. One day I had to decide whether to sign on or go to Mass. I decided to go to Mass. When I returned to the presbytery, there was a letter waiting for me. Inside the envelope was a note from a priest, thanking me for a retreat I had given and enclosing a cheque for four hundred pounds.

Damien, an Irish architect, was also living in the presbytery at St Joan of Arc. He was trying to discern his vocation while at the same time helping Father Fred draw up plans for improvements to the church. Like me, he was thinking of the religious life. We shared a lot together. A few days before I was due to go off to New York, we went for a walk.

'John, I'm not sure if I should enter religious life,' said Damien. He'd been accepted for postulancy by the Community of St John in France.

'Why?' I asked.

'Because I don't think I'm chaste enough.'

'What makes you say that?'

Looking very downcast, Damien went on to tell me that he'd been watching videos with sex scenes in them. They weren't porno videos, but mainstream movies – which in some cases are very pornographic, I believe.

I smiled to myself. 'Damien, I'll let you into a little secret.'

'What?'

'I've had exactly the same struggle, mate. I know how easy it is to give in to that temptation.' Then I told him about the nights when I used to stay up late watching Sky TV.

'So it's not just me, then,' he said with relief.

'No. A lot of people, if they were honest, would admit to similar struggles. Listen, you're as worthy to enter the priesthood as I am. God doesn't call you because you're perfect. We're all sinners, but he still loves us.'

One night, when Karen and I were sitting in my room talking, she grabbed me and began to kiss me passionately. I responded in the same way, and the two of us were soon writhing on top of the bed. Then we stopped suddenly, sat up and fell into an awkward silence. We both knew this wasn't right.

On the morning of my departure for New York, when I was gathering together my few possessions, Neil turned up to say goodbye. 'I love you, brother,' he said, 'and I'll be praying for you. Please pray for me.'

We gave each other a hug. I reflected that my time at Highbury had been very rewarding. Some parishioners were puzzled that I was going to try my vocation in America. I explained to them that I'd chosen to join an order in America because I couldn't find any religious communities in Britain that seemed to offer the kind of radical, sacrament-centred, prayerful life I was seeking. True, there were good men living in these communities, but the vision and the charisms of the founder had been lost somewhere. I needed a real challenge, one that would really test my faith and commitment.

Karen said goodbye to me at Arsenal tube station. She hugged me, told me how much she would miss me, and handed me a letter. I would miss her, too, but I knew God was calling me to the Friars. On the flight to New York, I took out her letter. I felt very emotional as I read it. She told me how much she loved me; how she'd never loved anyone as she'd loved me. Was I doing the right thing? I would soon find out.

Eleven

The Bronx

IT WAS SEPTEMBER 1998, I was thirty-four, and excited at beginning a new life as a postulant with the Franciscan Friars of the Renewal at the Friary of Our Lady of the Angels in the South Bronx. My room, which was on the second floor, was small and simply furnished with a bed and a desk. A large crucifix hung on the wall. Looking at all my worldly possessions – two pairs of grey trousers, two shirts, two pairs of socks, some underwear, a Bible, a rosary and a catechism – I felt liberated.

On that first night, I knelt down by my mattress and prayed that God would give me the grace to follow his will and be a good postulant. I particularly needed his help to curb my aggression and to give up smoking. The Friars didn't allow smoking.

There were nine other postulants: Edmund, whose family were from Lebanon or Syria; Andrew, a Syrian-rite Catholic, one of the Eastern Catholic Churches; Barry, who had been a bit of a hippy-type and a rebel and was from Kent; Kevin, a short guy with a ginger beard and a great sense of humour; Jim, a reserved but cheerful Texan; Sean and Scott, who were both very intense; Steve, who came from Queens and was the son of an NYPD cop; and Patrick, who was always moaning.

The regular community consisted of Father Conrad, the superior, who had spent a year in prison for his pro-life beliefs; Father Glen, who told me he'd been 'a bum working for a large TV network' before becoming a priest; Father Andrew and Father Bernard; Brother John Anthony, a former US Marine and mercenary; Brother Joseph and Brother Francis, formerly Troy. It was great to see Troy again, and he told me not to worry about my new life. 'If I can do it, John, so can you.'

From the beginning, I got on well with Brother Francis, Brother John Anthony and Brother Joseph. We were not just all around the same age, but we'd also come from similar backgrounds and had lived in darkness for part of our lives.

Brother Joseph reassured me cheerily about life in the friary, and told me that he understood my battle with nicotine as he too had been a smoker.

'Here's a few points, John, that will help you,' he said. 'Don't think of going out for a meal. You've got to forget all of that here.'

'And what about women?' I asked. September was a hot month in New York and, as I'd already noticed, some of the women in the Bronx didn't believe in leaving much to the imagination when they walked down the street.

'Well, what can I say?' he smiled. 'The best thing I can suggest is to keep your eyes on the pavement.'

Prayer, he continued, was essential if I was to live the life of a postulant successfully. Without it, I might as well forget religious life. Equally important was discipline, such as not being late for meals and not questioning the decisions of the superior. When it came to the psychological tests I would have to sit, he advised me to be honest and to the point, but not to say too much.

He warned me about wandering around the streets of the South Bronx alone, as some of the projects were no-go areas as a result of regular shootings, random violence and drug dealing. The friars, I learned, were safe when they wore their habits, because everyone knew who they were. But because postulants wore ordinary clothes, albeit a uniform of white shirts and grey trousers, they could be targets for muggers who would think they were tourists. It was, he said, safer to go out with a friar and always to wear sandals without socks.

There was a mixed feeling among the postulants as we

contemplated our new life and home. We felt a certain amount of excitement, along with a joy in knowing that we were all standing up for Christ, but we also felt some anxiety, given the austere life we would be expected to live and the obedience that would be demanded of us.

A typical day in the friary began at 5.30 a.m., if you wanted a shower. Each floor had just one shower, so if someone was in the one on your floor, you would have to go to another floor. If you got up at 5.50 a.m., which I did on several occasions, it was just a case of throwing some water on your face before hurrying downstairs to the chapel. The first office of readings began at 6 a.m. and finished at 6.30. Following this was an hour of silence, during which you could remain in the chapel, make a cup of coffee in the kitchen, go to your room to read, or sit in the courtyard outside.

Morning Prayer was said at 7.30 a.m., followed by Mass. After a quick breakfast of cereal and bagels, we were allocated jobs around the friary. The Friars had moved into the property about four years before, when a female religious community moved out. Much renovation had been done since then, but more was still needed. We were given tedious jobs to do around the place each day, such as removing the paint on the banisters and sanding them down. We were expected to find meaning in these lowly tasks. Sometimes I would be told to take care of some light fittings, which meant I would have to go out to a shop to buy bulbs. I loved being out. During the daytime it wasn't too dangerous.

We returned to the chapel for Midday Prayer. Lunch was at 12.30 p.m. The food was always very simple, often pasta or tinned fish. As the food became a bit monotonous after a while, I sometimes used to make pancakes – even though we were only supposed to have them on feast days.

In the afternoon we had classes in subjects such as Franciscan spirituality, catechism and, because of the ethnic composition of the South Bronx, Spanish. Between 4 and 5 p.m. you could read, write letters, go out or just sleep.

Holy hour was at 5 p.m., after which we had supper. Supper was more leisurely than lunch and would often go on until 7.30 p.m. Friars would take it in turns to read from the Church Fathers, St Francis or other lives of the saints. We were allowed to talk during the meal, but I used to find it very hard to sit there for up to an hour and a half, and I was always relieved when we trooped into the kitchen to do the washing up. We were free again until 9 p.m., when we returned to the chapel for Night Prayer and the rosary. At 10 p.m. silence was imposed until after Mass in the morning.

The Friars lived entirely off donations. In fact, this was one of the main reasons why I joined them – to rely only on the providence of God. They used to put much of the food in the freezer, so they always had something in store. They would buy items such as milk, fruit and vegetables when needed.

Each of the postulants was allocated a spiritual director. Mine was Father Andrew, who was in charge of the order and wrote books and gave retreats. I got on well with him. There was one downside to our meetings, however: because of his hectic workload, he would often fall asleep – not the most conducive thing when you're unburdening your soul and seeking spiritual guidance and support!

I soon discovered that life with the Friars was going to be much harder than I'd imagined. The order's formation programme was designed to mould the students into the Franciscan way of life. For someone like me, who had always considered himself very much an individual, and often naturally rebellious, this was a hard lesson to learn. Some mornings, kneeling in the chapel, I would panic at the thought that I was with the Friars for the rest of my life.

One day, in front of several other postulants, Father Conrad told me to go and park the minibus in the drive. I told him it had run out of oil. He ignored this and simply told me to go and park it up.

'But Father, it doesn't have any oil in. How can I park it?' I argued.

Raising his voice, he repeated again, 'Go and park the minibus.'

I walked away, confused and frustrated. That night, though, I remembered a story about St Francis instructing a brother to go out and plant cabbages upside down. When St Francis discovered that the brother had, in fact, planted them the right way up, he said, 'I didn't ask you for common sense. I asked you for obedience.' The next day I went and apologised to Father Conrad.

Living under such an austere regime after being used to life's little luxuries was not easy. One day, for example, someone sent me five dollars. I was excited at having some money of my own and wondered what I should do. I knew that I was expected to give it to the community, but the temptation was too much. I took the keys to the community's car, drove to a shop a few streets away, bought a tub of Häagen-Dazs ice cream and sat in the car savouring each mouthful. It had always tasted pretty good, but on this occasion it tasted absolutely fantastic. Needless to say, when I'd licked the last drop of ice cream from the spoon, guilt set in.

Most evenings, I would visit the Padre Pio homeless shelter at St Crispin's Friary, which was connected to Our Lady of the Angels by a courtyard. Around twenty men slept there each night. I was amazed at how spotless the place was. It looked like a hotel. The men slept in a dormitory and the sheets on each bed looked so white and crisp. The friars provided spiritually uplifting videos, CDs and chessboards. Unlike some other homeless shelters I've visited, there was no bad smell there.

When I asked Father Bob, one of the friars who worked at the shelter, why it was so clean and pleasant, he replied, 'Well, if you had Jesus coming to stay with you, wouldn't you make it as clean and comfortable as possible?'

What all this did was to give these men a dignity – a dignity they didn't have on the streets during the day. I learned so much from them. I remember one man, a black Baptist, who told me that the horrors he'd witnessed as a soldier in Vietnam had been responsible for the collapse of his marriage, his alcoholism and his eventual homelessness. He couldn't reconcile a loving, caring God with the evil he'd witnessed on the battlefields of Vietnam. I tried to explain that it was the evil in man, not God, that was responsible.

He believed in God, he said, but not the Church. He told me of the day when, in an attempt to try to change his life, he had walked into a Catholic church during Mass and had gone up to receive communion. However, because he was a tramp, the priest had refused to give him communion and offered a blessing instead. He was outraged by this: Jesus never refused anyone. I told him that all the priests I knew would give communion to anyone who came up to them, if they didn't know them. In this case the priest was judging him on his appearance. How often we all do that.

Sometimes I used to go on sandwich runs under the bridges along the Hudson River, where homeless people lived in cardboard boxes and tents and would sit around oil drums talking and drinking. It reminded me of the film *The Fisher King*, with Robin Williams. In fact, that film played a small part in my conversion, because I realised that it was really all about the mercy and forgiveness of Jesus.

A constant stream of people came to the friary for food. Most were Hispanic or black, and a number were on crack. We used to give out 'belly bombers' (puddings and cakes) and tea, coffee and soup. In order to prevent them from selling the tinned food they received as handouts, the friars made a point of removing the labels. What I saw most among these people was a real sense of hopelessness. I shared my story with some of the crack addicts, but I knew that unless they wanted to change, all we could do was to love them and provide food.

The friars also visited the homes of poor families, to see the conditions they lived in and then give them a card which enabled them to come to the friary to obtain food. I visited a number of these homes, which were in the projects, and was amazed to see that many had hardly a stick of furniture, as it had all been sold to buy drugs. Some people wore second-hand clothes, and the kids had few toys.

Around the South Bronx there were a lot of plaques on pavements and walls. On these would be sprayed the name of someone who had been killed. All the gang members wore scarves to identify which gang they belonged to. One day, through my bedroom window, I saw police carrying machine guns and wearing riot gear storm a house opposite. Apparently it was a crack house. Even though they were living in such a dangerous area, the friars had only minimal security at the friary and would open the door to anyone, no matter what time of day or night.

Despite the poverty and drugs in the South Bronx there was, unlike in Britain, a deep respect for God – as there seems to be in the USA as a whole. If you say 'God bless' to someone in America, they don't consider you odd, as people would in Britain. What's more, priests and religious are given much more respect. When I travelled on the subway and gave out Divine Mercy cards and talked to people about Jesus, I never encountered any hostility.

One major lesson I learned that year was not to despise the wealthy. I admit that I used to be very prejudiced against wealthy people. While I've never been into liberation theology, I still couldn't reconcile luxury with living out the Gospel. During my time with the Friars, however, I met some very wealthy New Yorkers who gave incredibly generously to the order's work. One woman, who was married to an extremely successful businessman, would donate regular cheques to the Friars and would also arrive with bags of groceries. I once went to their beautiful house on Long Island to take part in a prayer group. With its antique furniture, chandeliers, winding staircase and valuable oil paintings on the walls, it was like something out of the TV series *Dallas*.

I now believe there's nothing wrong in being wealthy; it's what you do with your wealth that matters. St Paul didn't say that money was the root of all evil, but that the love of money was. Over the years, I've met people consumed by greed and others with a desire to give generously to others. Jesus told a story about a rich man whose barns were packed with wheat and who wanted to build more barns to store more wheat. He used the story to make the point that the man didn't know when God would call for his soul.

When I received a phone call one day in November to say that my dad, who was on dialysis and had a heart condition, was critically ill and had been taken to hospital, I was very worried and spent the night in the chapel praying for him. I flew to London the next day. If he was going to die, I wanted to be there to tell him I loved him.

Dad was pleased to see me, and was quite upbeat about his condition. 'Don't worry, son, I'll pull through,' he said with a smile. I spent a week in London, staying with my mum, who was still coming to terms with Alan's death, and visiting my dad in hospital each day. Then I flew back to New York, but returned a few weeks later for the Christmas break, by which time Dad had improved greatly.

My time back in London gave me an opportunity to reflect on my life with the Friars. I still wasn't sure if this was the life for me, but I was going to give it my best shot. I'd known from the beginning that life with the Friars would be tough, and those I'd spoken to about my uncertainties had assured me that questioning was normal when you embarked on religious life.

Returning to the friary, I soon settled back into the daily routine of prayer, Mass, work and study. One morning at breakfast, Father Conrad announced that Mother Teresa was in New York and the community had been invited to attend Mass with her at the Missionaries of Charity house in the South Bronx. He told us that he had once remarked to her, 'Mother, every time I see you, you get smaller and smaller.'

She had replied, 'I am trying to be small enough to fit into the heart of Jesus.'

We were all excited as we piled into the minibus the next morning for the short journey to the Missionaries of Charity. Mother Teresa was, we all agreed, both a living saint and one of the greatest women of our time.

We soon arrived at the Missionaries of Charity house in a very run-down street of cheap shops, and took our places in the small, simple chapel along with about twenty Missionaries of Charity, many of them young Indian women. During the Mass, celebrated by Father Conrad and two other priests, I found it difficult to tear my eyes away from Mother's wrinkled face. She looked so serene and prayerful. When it came to the sign of peace, I should have followed the lead of the sisters and joined my hands and bowed. Instead, I found myself waving across to Mother, who grinned back at me.

After the Mass, we stayed in the chapel and listened to Mother Teresa talk to us about God's love. She then gave each of us a rosary, which has become one of my most treasured possessions. I met her on three other occasions, and each time I came away inspired by her simplicity and saintliness. She radiated the love of God.

Mother Teresa was, of course, one of the greatest campaigners against the evil of abortion. It might sound strange coming from a former gangster, but even before I found God, I was opposed to abortion. I felt life was life. In New York I joined some of the other community members in peaceful pro-life protests outside abortion clinics. One morning I prayed in the chapel before we set off for a vigil outside a clinic in the main shopping area of the South Bronx. I asked God that at least one woman might turn back from the doors of the clinic and so save the life of her unborn child. Up to this point, we had been unsuccessful in persuading any of the women to change their minds.

As usual, we stood outside the clinic praying the rosary. I was holding a large crucifix. A car pulled up and a woman got out of the passenger seat. She looked directly at the cross, paused, and then said to the man behind the wheel, 'Drive on,' and got back into the car.

I let out a prayer of thanks to God. But then I saw that the woman had simply got out of the car further down the street and was going into the clinic by the side entrance. I was devastated and found myself crying. I had thought that she'd had second thoughts after seeing the crucifix. When the woman came out a few hours later, I felt nothing but pity for her. Then I felt God say to me, 'If you are crying, how do you think I feel?'

On occasions, the atmosphere at these vigils became highly charged. Once I remember a policeman screaming at a seventy-year-old man that he had to move. The policeman grabbed the man and threw him across the pavement. When I saw this, my blood boiled and I felt a surge of anger against the violence of the policeman. I wanted to do him, but I managed to control myself.

The next day I brought up this incident with my spiritual director, Father Andrew. He told me that it was one of the devil's ploys to get a person to lose their temper. 'If there's anger, then God can't use you,' he said. 'You have to be filled with peace and love.'

He went on to recall the time when he told three doctors entering an abortion clinic that Jesus loved them and that he loved the babies they were going to kill. Within half an hour, the three of them came out, walked up to him and asked him to pray for them every day of his life, because they had decided not to carry out any more abortions.

Some people argue that vigils such as these should not be undertaken, as the women are going through a very traumatic experience. Yet this conveniently sidesteps one of the main issues, namely the suffering women experience after an abortion. As the famous American car sticker states, 'Abortion: one dead; one wounded.'

Counsellors would always try to encourage the women to

keep their baby, and even offer financial help. Most women, however, ignored these pleas. Since that time, I've done post-abortion counselling and have met women crushed by the guilt of having had an abortion. Many said to me that they now wanted to hold that child. The vigils were always carried out in a spirit of love, not condemnation. When the women emerged from the clinic after an abortion, we would reassure them that Jesus loved them and that he would forgive them if they asked him to.

Some who call themselves 'pro-lifers' have fire-bombed clinics and shot doctors. I would never go down this road, as my response is always based on what I feel Jesus wants me to do. Jesus wouldn't fire-bomb a clinic or take out a gun. I believe that only love and prayer, not anger and hatred, will persuade a woman to reverse her decision to have an abortion.

In February I had a chat with Father Conrad to find out what sort of progress I was making as a postulant. He said I was doing fine, but there were a couple of things he wanted to talk to me about.

'You need to get on top of your backchatting,' he said. 'You have a tendency, sometimes, to go off on a tangent in a conversation.' He paused and then added, 'I can imagine you with a pint of beer and being a real thug.'

I was stunned. I'd left that life behind me, and over the last few years I'd tried my best to live as a Christian. How could he see me as a thug? I left his office feeling downcast, confused and angry.

Three days later, he asked to see me again. He told me that he had serious doubts about my vocation as a friar and didn't think, at the moment, that I was suitable for the noviciate. He said that my back, which had been causing me problems for a while, also made me unsuitable. What's more, he told me that if I was in a group, I would bring myself down to their level. And he didn't feel I'd learned sufficient obedience during my time at the friary.

'You need to pray to find out if you have a vocation to the

Friars, John,' he said. 'You need to take some time out. I want you to take a month and really pray and reflect about whether it's God's will for you to be here.'

Initially I felt angry with Father Conrad. I'd joined the Friars expecting to be there for the rest of my life. I'd given up everything. One day I went to see Father Glen, hoping to find encouragement and support. I wasn't disappointed. Father Glen listened intently as I unburdened myself. At the end of it, he suggested I gave myself two more weeks at the friary and prayed to God for guidance. His words produced a sense of freedom inside me.

'Your will be done, not mine,' was my prayer each day. One day, when I was kneeling in the chapel, I saw a picture in my mind. First of all I saw a wall with a wounded child behind it, and then I saw that the wall had been knocked down. Then, in my room one evening, I heard the words, 'Embrace the child.' I felt the Holy Spirit go right through me. When I opened the Bible I saw the words, 'Go home, your servant is healed.' I realised then that I had been healed. It became apparent to me that I'd joined the Friars not because God wanted me to be a friar, but because I wanted to be holy. God had used the experience to heal me and make me a better person.

That year, Pope John Paul II visited the USA and twelve of us travelled in a minibus to attend a Mass in a hockey stadium in St Louis, Missouri. Being at the Mass with an ecstatic crowd of twenty thousand was an incredible experience, and reminded me of the tremendous fervour I'd witnessed at the World Youth Day in Paris. I remember one young girl shouting out at one point, 'JP, I love you!' The pope stopped in mid-sentence, smiled, and said, 'I think I love you more.'

The pope radiated so much love and joy. After listing all the evils in the world – drugs, abortion, poverty, promiscuity – he then said, 'You young people in America are the light of

Christ. And darkness cannot stand the light. So burn for Christ!' At that, a huge roar went up.

When I came out of the stadium, I noticed a young girl standing near a hot-dog stand, giving out anti-Catholic leaflets and booklets. Walking up to her, I asked, 'Do you know what the pope was talking about in the stadium?'

'No,' she replied.

'Well, I've just been listening to him. He was talking about unity between all the churches, so that they could be one voice crying out against all the evil in the world. And here you are, attacking the Catholic Church. Let me ask you: are you against abortion?'

'Of course I am,' she answered.

'Well, the pope was talking about the evil of abortion and how it destroys the world.' I then listed other topics the pope had talked about: materialism, euthanasia, social justice, human rights, etc. 'But you're trying to turn people away from his voice. If we all worked together, the world would be a better place.'

She went silent, and nodded.

'Can I ask you if you prayed about this protest?' I asked.

'Well, no,' she said, 'but we believe that we are the true Church.'

'I'm not asking that. I'm asking if you prayed.' I also pointed out that Catholics didn't picket the meetings of her Church.

To my surprise, she put her leaflets into a bag and walked away. She had realised that she was fighting against what she actually believed in.

Once I had made up my mind to leave the Friars, I decided to spend a week preparing for life back in England at Trinity House on Long Island, a large house where priests go for retreats. It's also the base of Father Benedict Groeschel, who was responsible for founding the Franciscan Friars of the Renewal and is a renowned preacher and writer.

Father Benedict listened as I explained that I'd made the decision to leave the Friars. He told me to trust in God and

147

that God would bless me when I returned to England. 'John,' he said, 'you're a free spirit and God will use you as a free spirit.'

Twelve

The Holy Land

I ARRIVED BACK AT HEATHROW one day in March 1999, and caught the tube over to my mum's place in Leyton. I was pleased to see that she was getting her life back together after Alan's death. She was now very involved with the St Vincent de Paul Society, was a member of the parish prayer group and had made lots of new friends.

It seemed strange being away from the structured life of the friary. I didn't know what the future held, but I was confident that God would direct me. The Friars had given me nine hundred pounds to get myself set up again, so for once I didn't have any immediate financial worries.

After a couple of days with my mum and several visits to my dad, who was now back home and looking well, I went for a few days' retreat to the Family House of Prayer. Walking among the hills and kneeling at night in the chapel, I reflected that I'd made the right decision in leaving the Friars.

On the way back to London, I stopped off in Leeds to see Robert Toone of Youth 2000. As we sat in his house in East Keswick, I told him that I didn't know what God was calling me to do. Robert asked me now if I would like to spend a year giving retreats in schools around Britain. When I told him I wasn't sure, he suggested we pray about it.

We began the rosary. When we reached the third mystery, Robert prayed out loud, 'As you said to the centurion, "Go home, your servant is healed", we ask you to heal us.' I was stunned. This was exactly the reading I'd received in my room at the friary when I was contemplating my future outside the order. Robert didn't know this, of course.

At the end of the rosary, I said, 'Robert, I've made up my mind. That reading you had is the same one I had just before I left the Friars.'

He looked at me and smiled. 'Great, John. It will be a blessed year for you.'

I phoned Neil, whom I'd first met on that retreat in Ilford and who had since become a Youth 2000 volunteer, and asked if he wanted to spend a year on the road with me. He thought it sounded like a great idea.

Our first task was to visit the village of Walsingham in Norfolk, where Youth 2000 were to have a major five-day retreat in August. Robert had asked me whether we should hold the event at Worth Abbey in West Sussex or Walsingham. Worth had excellent facilities, but could only take four hundred people. What's more, it would cost fifty pounds a head. Many in Youth 2000 felt that we should use Worth. Robert, however, felt that Our Lady wanted the event held in Walsingham, England's national Marian shrine.

Youth 2000 were hoping to attract about one and a half thousand young people to the retreat, which would be the largest gathering of its kind since the visit of Pope John Paul to Britain in 1982, so I was told. At that time, I was heavily into a life of crime, of course, and wasn't even aware that the pope was in Britain. Neither Neil nor I had ever been involved in organising an event as big as this, and we knew that the logistics would be a nightmare and there were many things that could go wrong.

A lady called Janey, who lived with her non-Catholic husband in a beautiful converted barn, kindly agreed to put us up for a couple of days. She introduced us to the parish priest, and also to some local women, who said that they would pray for the success of the event. She also introduced us to a farmer who said we could use some of his fields for tents, for just a thousand pounds. We contacted a tent hire company and booked the tents, then went round the village and booked up a number of rooms in the bed and breakfast places. The director of the Catholic shrine agreed to let us use it. We also had to contact the police and fire brigade because of the number of people involved.

It was all slightly unnerving. The tents alone would cost about twenty-two thousand pounds. What if hardly anyone turned up for the event? How would we pay for it? But Neil and I trusted in God. If he, and Our Lady, wanted the event to succeed, then it would.

In order to generate interest in the retreat, we visited a number of schools and encouraged as many youngsters as possible to come along. When we returned to Walsingham in August, three days before the retreat was due to begin, we were both amazed by what we saw. Robert had pulled together a team of volunteers and they had done a superb job in getting the site ready and putting in place everything that was needed. The tents and marquees had been erected, the stage and sound system set up and the Portaloos delivered.

The five-day retreat went like a dream and the weather was hot and sunny. The young people arrived on coaches from most major cities in Britain. Some looked bored and uncomfortable as they made their way to their tents. They clearly weren't sure what to expect. Some were probably fearful that they might have let themselves in for a spot of Bible bashing – and out here in the middle of the Norfolk countryside, there would be nowhere to run to if their fears were confirmed. I knew, however, that they were going to have a great experience of the love of God. I'd seen this happen so many times at schools and on retreats.

There were forty-five priests present, and there was perpetual adoration each day. With amazement in his voice, one priest told me after the retreat that from 8 a.m. until 8 p.m. each day he had done nothing else but hear confessions. I reckon that the vast majority of the one and a half thousand young people there went to confession. For some, it was the first time in years.

One afternoon, I left the main tent for a quick ciggy break. Standing outside, looking depressed, was a young girl called Alex. I spoke to her and asked her how she was finding the retreat. She looked startled. I could sense an awful lot of pain in her. We began to chat, and as we did she opened up. I was shocked to hear that she'd made three suicide attempts in her life. Her mother was an alcoholic, she revealed, and her stepfather had abused her. Then she told me that she didn't think someone like me would take the trouble to talk to her. Puzzled, I asked her what she meant.

'Well, you're someone very important up there on the stage,' she said. 'I just didn't think you would want to talk to me.'

She saw me as a glamorous figure simply because I was standing on the stage with a microphone. I told her I was no one special and that I too had been through really dark periods – until God entered my life.

We talked a lot, and she went away feeling much lighter, it seemed. Later she wrote to Youth 2000 to say that her conversation with me had changed her life. She is now full of joy and peace. Her life is still not great in many ways, but she knows that God is with her.

My time giving talks and leading retreats has taught me that you just never know what kind of effect you have on people. I've tried to see my work as that of a sower, scattering seeds of hope and faith along the way. The same applies when we say destructive things to people. Just as those words of hope and faith can build people up, so negative and hurtful words can break people and damage them.

When they left Walsingham at the end of that retreat, many young people were singing and dancing or hugging each other. It was brilliant, as if waves of joy were being released across the country. A number of people came up to me as they were about to get onto their coach and said that I'd changed their lives. I always replied, 'It wasn't me, it was God. And it was in spite of me.'

Robert suggested that Neil and I should go away for two weeks to recharge our spiritual batteries and have a bit of a holiday. We weren't sure where to go, however. We thought about Rome, Assisi and San Giovanni. Then Neil suggested the Holy Land. We prayed about this, and felt it was the right decision.

While we were giving retreats at some schools in Wales, we'd met a woman who was so impressed by our work that she offered to pay for a holiday for us. She suggested we went to Medjugorje, but Neil and I had both been there already, so we didn't take her up on the offer. Now, hoping that she hadn't forgotten us, I phoned her and she kindly agreed to pay for our flights to the Holy Land. We would have to pay for our own accommodation and find our own spending money. Delighted, we booked the flights. But what were we going to do when we got there? Where would we stay? What would we eat? As usual, we placed our trust in God and prayed about it.

A week later, as we were driving to Downside Abbey in Somerset to set up a retreat, a hitchhiker flagged us down. We stopped, and he told us where he wanted to go. Even though it wasn't on our way, we decided to give him a lift. We arrived at a nearby town, and he said he would get the bus from there – but could we give him the eight pounds for the fare? Apart from our petrol money, we only had ten pounds between us, but we gave it to him.

We spent a night at Downside and joined the monks the next morning for Morning Prayer in the chapel. Just as we were leaving, Father Michael gave us some money in an envelope, stressing that it was for us, as he knew how hard we worked. When we opened the envelope, we found a cheque for five hundred pounds in it. Neil and I looked at each other and, thinking of the hitchhiker, we remembered the words in the gospel, that whatever you give you will get back tenfold.

The following week we flew to Israel. At Tel Aviv airport we hired a car and set off towards Jerusalem, a little worried that we now only had a hundred and twenty pounds to cover the two weeks and no accommodation lined up. We parked the car in Arab East Jerusalem, a chaotic part of the city that seemed to be one big traffic jam, and went in search of a hotel.

A scruffy Arab man sitting outside a café near the bus station called us over and said he had a lovely hotel that was quite cheap. 'It very good. You like. Come.'

We followed him through the crowded streets, where Israeli soldiers patrolled, to a run-down building in a narrow alley in the Old City. When we saw the room, our hearts sank. It was filthy, and had green mould on the wall. What's more, it was fifteen pounds a night. We told the man we would think about it, but we had no intention of returning.

We thought we might find something more suitable and affordable if we went to one of the many religious orders which offer accommodation. We were astonished to discover, however, that they were more expensive than the hotels. A number of them turned us away because we weren't with a pilgrimage group. Neil and I were incensed by this. We felt that we were true pilgrims, and had expected a religious order to welcome us in that spirit.

I remember walking into the reception of one Christian hostel and discovering that it was double the price of a normal hotel. When the manager said he couldn't help us, I replied sarcastically, 'Jesus would be proud of you.'

At another hostel, we received the same response. 'What would you do if it was Jesus knocking at the door?' I said to the nun who ran it.

'You're making me feel guilty,' she replied.

'Good. You should feel guilty,' I said sharply. 'You set up these places in the Holy Land, and yet you don't put up poor pilgrims who've come for one reason only: to live Jesus and to go back strengthened to evangelise. We're true disciples. We don't own anything.'

She looked at me, unsure of what to say, and turned away.

I could really feel what it must have been like for Joseph and Mary when they journeyed to Bethlehem. Were they angry? I know I was. We must have gone to over twenty religious houses, and each one refused to put us up. In addition, Neil, who is diabetic, was feeling low because of the incredible heat. In the end, we returned to the dingy hotel in the Old City and booked in for the night.

The next day, we decided to drive the five miles to Bethlehem to see if the Rosary Sisters could put us up. A woman at the information office had recommended them. In a café in the Old City we met two American priests who, we learned, were also on their way to Bethlehem. We offered them a lift, for which they were very grateful. The taller of the two priests reminded us that it was the Feast of the Holy Rosary, and said it was the day on which he was born and the day on which he was ordained. And now, here we were on our way to meet the Rosary Sisters.

When we arrived at the large convent in the centre of Bethlehem, the sisters welcomed us warmly and immediately asked the two priests if they would celebrate Mass for them in the chapel. It was very moving. All the thirty or so sisters were Arab, and many of them were quite young. Also present were eighteen young Palestinian girls who were living with them while they thought about entering religious life. I found this inspiring. The Rosary Sisters were the first religious order we'd found in the country whose main aim was to provide hospitality to poor pilgrims, not to make money.

After unpacking, we went with the priests to visit the Church of the Nativity in Manger Square, which was full of coaches and groups of tourists clutching cameras. There must have been a couple of hundred people queuing up to get into the Holy Sepulchre through the tiny door, known as the Door of Humility.

I went up to an elderly Greek Orthodox priest and told him that the two American priests wanted to see where Jesus was born. Without further ado, he led us through a separate entrance into the dark church and then, unhitching a rope, took us down the steps into the Grotto of the Nativity where Jesus was born.

'Stay here as long as you want,' he said, hooking the rope back and then disappearing.

We couldn't believe it. Here we were, in the spot where Jesus was born, and separated from the crowds of pilgrims by a rope. I experienced an incredible feeling of being united with Jesus. Looking at the fourteen-pointed silver star embedded in white marble, I found myself reflecting on the miracle of God entering the world as a helpless baby. I was also struck by how God was so dependent on Mary and Joseph. We decided to pray the rosary. When it came to the third joyful mystery, the birth of Jesus, the taller priest was so moved that he began to cry: it was the Feast of the Holy Rosary, the day of his birth and ordination, and he was in the place where Jesus was born.

For many non-Catholics, the honour Catholics give to Mary can be a stumbling block. But the reason why Mary is so important to Catholics is that God honoured her so much by entrusting his only son to her care. The salvation of the entire world was placed in Mary's hands.

Later that evening, Neil and I spent three hours praying in the convent chapel. The sisters were amazed at two young blokes spending so much time in prayer. In fact, I think they thought we were the holiest people they'd met!

The mother superior told us it didn't matter that we didn't have much money, and said we could stay at the convent as long as we liked. She even said the sisters would make us packed lunches when we went out for the day, and if we wanted to travel to other parts of the Holy Land she would arrange for us to stay with the nearest group of Rosary Sisters.

Before leaving for the Holy Land, I'd been told about a remarkable orphanage run by Polish nuns on the Mount of Olives. Neil and I decided to pay a visit. When we arrived at the orphanage, at the top of a rough road and with a spectacular view of Jerusalem, a smiling nun welcomed us and offered to show us around. She explained that the nuns had been given the land by King Hussein of Jordan during the Six Day War. Some years later, the nuns built an orphanage for Palestinian children.

We were introduced to Mother Raphael, a remarkable and inspiring woman. When we explained that we were evangelists working with Catholic young people, she asked us to talk to the children, who were very curious to know who we were. Mother gathered the children together in the dining room and motioned us to begin. We spoke about how God loved them and how valued they were, then concluded our talk by singing a song. It was so sad to look at those young faces and know that these children were being brought up in an orphanage, not with their parents. As soon as we'd finished, the children burst into a song to Our Lady in Arabic.

I remember one beautiful little girl with the most amazing eyes. I gave her a Padre Pio card and told her that Our Lady had a special place for her. She asked Mother Raphael if she could accept the card. Mother nodded and told me that the girl liked to be the best and liked to win everything. 'I've tried to explain to her that she doesn't need to win everything; she just needs to take part.' The little girl appeared to be a bit downcast at these words. Then Mother added, 'But we love her.' At this the little girl leapt up and hugged her. It was a beautiful sight.

As we were leaving, we met the most beautiful-looking nun digging in the garden. She smiled at us and then pointed to her face. 'This not beautiful,' she said. Then she held out her hands, which were caked in mud, and said, 'These are beautiful because they glorify God.'

A few days later we said our goodbyes to the Rosary Sisters in Bethlehem and set off for the port of Haifa, where we were to stay with another group of Rosary Sisters. Neil and I spent a day on the beach, which was wonderfully relaxing. We felt God was rejoicing in us playing in the sea.

Early the next morning, under a clear blue sky, we drove to Nazareth up in the hills of Galilee. We arrived at the modern Basilica of the Annunciation, which dominates the shabby-looking town, at 7 a.m. As we were walking around the outside of the church, an Arab Franciscan priest came up to us and asked us to follow him.

He led us silently into the empty church. Along the walls of the cloister were mosaics donated by Catholic communities around the world. Unlocking a gate, he motioned us down into the Grotto of the Annunciation and then disappeared. A few minutes later, he returned fully vested and proceeded to celebrate Mass in English.

It was an amazing experience to receive the body of Christ in the place where Jesus had grown up. Neil and I both welled up with tears. Afterwards, I asked the priest how he'd been able to celebrate Mass for us.

'Well, this is the Holy Land, so I told holy lies,' he chuckled. 'I said you were both seminarians.'

Our fortnight in the Holy Land was both refreshing and enriching. We met some inspiring people, and the Bible came alive in a new way. Prior to going, I'd only had blurred images of places such as Bethlehem, Jerusalem and Nazareth, and little idea of the climate, geography and culture. Now, having walked through the crowded, narrow streets of the Old City, with peasant women sitting outside the gates selling figs, grapes and bread, and having travelled along the winding, mountainous roads and walked through the hills of Galilee, I could imagine what it must have been like in the time of Jesus.

As soon as we arrived back at Stansted, Neil and I turned

our thoughts to the drive north to Ampleforth Abbey in North Yorkshire, where we'd been booked to lead a retreat for fifty boys at the school. The holiday was over. We were back on the road again.

Thirteen

On the road

WHEN NEIL AND I WENT INTO SCHOOLS to lead retreats, the kids were always surprised that two blokes like us should be standing in front of them talking about the love of God. We just didn't fit the kind of stereotype they had in their minds. At one school, a kid came up to me and said, 'You two are the last people I'd expected to be talking about God. You don't look the type. You look normal.' I laughed to myself when I heard this.

RE teachers would often contact Youth 2000 to say that, as a result of the retreat we'd led, some of the kids had been to Mass and confession for the first time in several years. I remember one teacher saying that Neil and I had done more in forty-five minutes than he'd achieved in seven years in the classroom.

The aim of these retreats was quite simply to bring young people into a personal understanding and experience of Jesus' love for them through the Eucharist, Our Lady and the teachings of the Church. We would have the rosary, Mass, a holy hour and all-night adoration. Neil, myself and others would give our testimony about the power of Jesus, and invited speakers would give talks about spirituality and Church teaching. Several of the Franciscan Friars of the Renewal, who often visited Britain for several weeks, joined us on some of the retreats and made a deep impression on the kids. Teachers, social workers and youth workers involved with Youth 2000 helped us to look after the kids. If we had fifty kids on a retreat, we would generally have five leaders. The kids usually slept in classrooms.

The first talk would be about the presence of Jesus in the Blessed Sacrament, and the second would be about the healing power of confession – or the sacrament of reconciliation, as it is now often called. At the end of each retreat we would give the kids some survival tips for when they returned to their parishes: pray for at least ten minutes each day, go to Mass and confession, read the Bible daily, and get involved in parish activities such as prayer groups or catechetical groups. We always urged the kids to live in the real world, but to live in it with Jesus. We stressed that it doesn't matter how many times we fall. God only asks that we try and that we seek his forgiveness. Mother Teresa said we should make our lives beautiful for God.

I remember one kid at a school in Preston coming up to me before Mass and saying, 'I don't want to go. It's boring. What's the point of it?'

'I used to find it boring,' I replied. 'But it's like a football match. If you don't get involved, you *will* find it boring. Have you asked God if that piece of bread is really him? I did, and now I don't find Mass boring.'

Our retreats were – and had to be – rooted in prayer. We spent an hour at the beginning and end of each day in prayer. We also visited a number of convents and monasteries, such as the Poor Clares, Carmelites and Carthusians, and asked them to pray for the success of our work.

One day, Neil and I decided on impulse to drive to Glastonbury in Somerset. We parked the car in the main street and went in search of the local Catholic church. There was a notice outside the church saying that adoration of the Blessed Sacrament took place every week. We knocked on the presbytery door, and a cheerful-looking priest opened it and introduced himself as Father Kevin. We told him who we were, and he invited us in. We were amazed when he said that he'd been expecting us. He wanted a retreat in his parish centre, he went on. Would we agree to do it? Without thinking, we said yes.

A few weeks later we arrived back in Glastonbury on a Friday afternoon, accompanied by Father Glen from the Friars of the Renewal. The parish priest had done a great job in promoting the retreat. Around a hundred and twenty young people were waiting in the parish centre when we turned up that evening.

Glastonbury is well known as a centre of the occult. Father Kevin had told us about a coven of witches who had booked the parish centre under false pretences. Needless to say, when he discovered who they were, he cancelled the booking. I don't know why it's such a centre for occult activities, given that the town has deep Christian roots. Legend says that Joseph of Arimathea, the man who gave the tomb to Christ, came to Glastonbury to convert the British and that he placed the Holy Grail, the cup Christ used at the Last Supper, beneath a spring on Tor Hill, east of the town. Joseph is said to have built a chapel at Glastonbury. In around AD 700 an abbey was founded, and it became one of the most famous in England. Glastonbury also has strong connections with King Arthur. Tor Hill is said by some to be the legendary Avalon, where his body was buried.

Well aware of Glastonbury's occult links, Neil and I had planned to hold a Blessed Sacrament procession through its streets. Father Kevin had thought this an excellent idea and had promised to clear it with the local police. On Sunday morning, however, he told us sheepishly that he'd forgotten to do this. We decided to hold the procession anyway. To contact the police at this late stage would almost certainly bring about a refusal.

As we walked slowly through the town, we attracted a great deal of interest from tourists and locals alike. Some local Catholics, touched by the sight of a hundred and twenty young people singing 'Hosanna in the highest', fell to their knees in the street. We gave out rosaries and Miraculous Medals along the way. We even offered them to the owners of some occult and New Age shops. To our surprise, they accepted them. We put this reaction down to the amount of grace that had been built up during the retreat. It was too powerful for any evil influences that might have been present.

A few weeks later, Neil and I were back in the West Country giving a talk in a secondary school in Taunton. Out of what must have been a thousand pupils, only one, a twelve-year-old boy, asked to come on a retreat. His name was Alan, and he wasn't even Catholic. He was living with foster parents and he hadn't had an easy life. Most of his childhood had been spent in the care of Social Services or foster parents. When he asked to come on the retreat, I told him that I would have to approach Social Services to get permission for him to come, and they might refuse.

'I really want to go,' Alan pleaded. 'Please don't let them say no.'

I contacted the local Social Services office and went along the next day to meet with Alan's key worker. After listening to me, she said she would have to speak to Alan and carry out a police check on me. Soon afterwards, she wrote to Youth 2000 to say that permission had been granted. When I phoned Alan with the news, he was overjoyed.

For Alan, that retreat was a moment of grace. It happened one evening in the chapel when a priest blessed him with the Blessed Sacrament. I was standing next to him, and when I looked down at him I saw the tears beginning to run down his face. I felt Jesus tell me to hug him. As I did, Alan buried himself in my chest, sobbing. I really felt his pain. He also went to confession, which gave him a great sense of freedom. He told me afterwards that it was the first time in his life that he realised he was truly loved.

Not long before Christmas, I gave a retreat for two hundred and fifty young people, over half of them wanting to be Youth 2000 leaders, at a centre in Galway, Ireland. During the retreat an Irish bishop warned the young people not to be jumping from one retreat to another, but to go out and evangelise

Ireland, where Catholicism has been much weakened in recent years. It was great to hear a bishop preach with such passion.

Predictably, as the Millennium Eve drew closer, the media hype increased. Amidst all the talk of the Dome, fireworks displays, pubs and restaurants planning to charge a fortune, one element seemed to be missing, namely Jesus Christ, the man behind the celebrations. Youth 2000 felt it was important to mark the true meaning of those two thousand years in a major way. The original plan was to stage an all-night vigil at Westminster Cathedral in London. Unfortunately, the cathedral had already been booked up. Someone suggested we try the Metropolitan Cathedral of Christ the King in Liverpool. Archbishop Patrick Kelly enthusiastically agreed to the event, and allowed us to run a retreat in the crypt during the week leading up to Millennium Eve.

From November until the last week of December, Neil and I worked flat out leading retreats in Liverpool, doing talks in schools and parishes and sending out posters and fliers. This promotion work was vital if we were to fill the cathedral. We had no idea how many young people would turn up.

The Millennium Eve event turned out to be incredible. Around two thousand seven hundred young people packed the cathedral. They could have chosen to go to pubs, clubs or parties, but instead they came to pray. During the night, priests placed at strategic points around the cathedral heard confessions. One priest there told me he had heard fourteen confessions that night. He added that the shortest period someone had been without the sacrament had been ten years, and the longest fifty-four years. The Franciscan Friars of the Renewal judge the success or failure of a retreat on the number of people who go to confession. By making a confession, you are saying to God, 'I want to start again.' And, as I always say, it's never too late to start again, and again, and again.

I think the highlight of the vigil for me was seeing Alan baptised. It was a very emotional moment to watch this young boy set out on his Christian journey. Neil and I were his godfathers. Since then, I've watched Alan grow in faith and become a much less broken human being.

Archbishop Patrick Kelly and I had been asked to talk to BBC Radio 5 Live. Standing in one of the side chapels, I listened to the archbishop. 'Some people out there tonight will be drinking in the new millennium, but we are praying in the new millennium,' he said. 'And I know which of the two is the better.'

When the reporter turned to me, I said, 'For all you people out there who don't know the love and mercy of Jesus, believe that he is waiting for you. And for any young people listening, come along to the cathedral tonight. It's the biggest party you will ever have. And it's better than waking up in the morning with a hangover.'

That Radio 5 interview was one of many I gave during that year on the road. Fascinated by my radical change of life from gangster to evangelist, a number of radio stations, as well as ITV's Sunday programme, asked to interview me, while articles about me appeared in several newspapers, including *The Times*. This was completely new to me. I knew little about the way the media worked and what they were looking for. I was fortunate in having Clare Ward to coach me. Before joining Youth 2000, she had worked as a journalist, including a stint at BBC Radio Leeds. She talked me though the interview process and explained how the interviewer and the subject often had different agendas. Her advice was, 'Think about what you want to say and say it, and don't let the interviewer lead you off down the garden path.'

By now, I was beginning to get a bit of a name for myself. My criminal background was a source of endless fascination for many people. There's a certain mystique about gangsters and the underworld. People want to know what it's like to live like that. It's a world most people only read about or glimpse in films, after all. When you become a celebrity of any description, however, even one in the retreat world, there's always a danger of it going to your head. When you're doing God's work this is particularly dangerous, as Neil warned me one night after a retreat. Without realising it, you can become the important one rather than God. God humbled me several times, I remember, and still does.

While Neil and I were staying with some friends in Manchester, for example, a woman asked me if I would give a talk in her local parish. She had told her parish priest about me and he had agreed. Of course, I said, feeling very bountiful as I accepted. I had a message for people – and, looking back, I know I wanted their affirmation and praise. I was on fire with the Holy Spirit. Or so I thought.

A couple of nights later I went to the church with the woman. We arrived a quarter of an hour before Mass so that she could introduce me to the parish priest. We found him in the sacristy. After we'd been introduced, I asked him if I could speak before the final blessing. If my talk was within the Mass, people would be more likely to stay.

I sat there after communion, keen to get up to the sanctuary and begin my talk. There were, I suppose, about fifty people in the church. As the priest stood up and began the concluding prayer, I edged along to the end of the bench. I was just about to step out into the aisle when he gave the final blessing. My heart sank. I was now like a sprinter on the starting blocks. Seconds were crucial if I was to have any kind of an audience. By habit, most Catholics immediately head for the door as soon as they've received the final blessing.

'You have all done your duty now,' said the priest, 'but if anyone wants to stay, we've got some chap here with us who wants to talk to you about a retreat.' With that, he glided across the sanctuary and through the door into the sacristy. As I strode swiftly up the aisle, the parishioners began to leave their benches and move in the opposite direction. This was going to be a disaster. I could see it.

Once my feet hit the sanctuary I introduced myself, but all I could see was the backs of people's heads, apart from the woman who'd brought me and a couple of elderly women in one of the front rows. They were praying the rosary, however.

'Excuse me!' I bellowed. 'Could you all please do me the courtesy of sitting down?' People stopped in their tracks and a few reluctantly shuffled into the nearest bench and sat down. I gave my talk, but the fire had gone out of me. At the end, I thanked everyone and left the sanctuary deflated. That night, when I prayed, I realised that God had taught me an important lesson in humility. I was not the special person; God was.

Wherever we went, there was an incredible grace. Neil and I both had to make sure that the message we preached was not one that would gain us popularity, but one that God wanted us to preach. And if you speak the words of Christ, there will be those who don't like it.

Despite our ministry, we were still simply single men, prone to all the normal temptations. We hadn't taken a vow of celibacy, although we were, of course, bound by Christ's teaching on chastity. Because we were telling many young girls and women in schools and on retreats how beautiful and precious they were, some, I think, developed crushes on us. Neil and I were both young, confident, witty and, in their eyes perhaps, charismatic. We had to pray hard in order to fight against lust. At the start of our year on the road, we had both made a commitment not to enter into a relationship with a woman. If anyone wants to know how hard this can be at times, just imagine yourself being doted on everywhere you go by extremely attractive members of the opposite sex. It's not easy, I can tell you.

I remember one eighteen-year-old girl, whom I'd met at a couple of retreats, asking me to visit her at home. She told me her parents were away. I felt excited at the prospect of meeting her, as I knew she liked me. On the way there, however, I asked God why I was going to see her. The word 'lust' came to me. I prayed to find out whether I should go, and I felt God saying to me that I should go, but to help her, not to use her. I did that, through God's strength.

From one day to the next, I never knew where we were going to be staying, how we were going to eat, or where we were going to get money to buy the basics and, in my case, ciggies. Yet during that year, Neil and I never went without a meal or a bed for the night. God always provided. I felt like one of the early apostles.

We used to get extremely tired, though, and when you're spending so much time with someone, disagreements, arguments and misunderstandings do take place. We had decided to have regular open confession with each other. Believe me, this was painful at times. If we were going to be really open and honest with each other – warts and all – we had to be able to trust each other. We all tend to wear disguises and hide bits of ourselves, because we fear rejection. Learning to trust isn't easy, as I well knew.

Like any organisation, Youth 2000 had within it people who had opposing views on the way things should be done. There were those who advocated what I would call the disco approach to youth retreats. To them I always replied flatly, 'Conversions don't happen at discos. When parishes run discos, they're saying, "Come to the world and we will give you a bit of Jesus." The Youth 2000 message is, "We will give you Jesus and you can live in the world with him." ' This is the only way to find true peace.

One day in the Youth 2000 office in Leeds, after a heated argument about retreats, Robert turned to me and said, 'John, you know it's not what you say – it's the way you say it. Try to be a bit more tactful.'

'I know, Robert,' I replied, 'but we're all flogging our guts out. And some of these leaders are only concerned with going to retreats, getting filled up with the Holy Spirit, going back home and then doing as little as possible. It gets my goat.'

He nodded sympathetically. 'Just try to say things a bit differently, John. I agree with a lot of what you're saying. But, at the end of the day, divisions are not created by God. And we're all at different stages of our journey.'

He was right, of course.

Neil and I used to go for spiritual direction to Father Denis Herlihy at St John the Baptist, Timperley, in Cheshire. A very wise and holy man, he seemed to know intuitively what was going on in our lives and where we needed special guidance.

One day we told him that we felt we were being attacked by the devil, as a number of things were going wrong and we seemed impatient with each other. Father Herlihy told us that he had once been asked by a man at a retreat if he believed in the devil. 'Yes,' he replied. 'What do you do about it?' asked the man. Father Herlihy realised that up until then, he hadn't given much thought to the devil. After that, he said, he prayed regularly for protection. 'Know the devil is real, but don't give him too much credit. Pray for protection,' he urged us.

When our year on the road came to an end, we agreed that it had been absolutely incredible. I'd had struggles, but I'd grown in faith and had learned to put more trust in God. Neil and I must have spoken to over seventy-five thousand young people across the country. We knew that we had scattered many seeds of faith along the way. When you preach the words of Christ, some people may take those words immediately and act to change their lives. For others, it may happen years down the line. Jesus' parable of the sower tells us that those seeds are received in many different ways.

Robert wanted me to stay on for another year with Youth 2000, but I told him I felt called by God to other work and to a time of personal inner healing. I was also burned out after such a hectic year of giving retreats all over the country, as well as in Ireland and Germany.

In April, I began work as a parish youth worker at St Austin's, a Benedictine parish in Grassendale, Liverpool. Father Justin, the parish priest, had asked me to help him set up a Life Teen programme. The aim of the programme, which originated in the USA, is to make young people feel a part of the church through vibrant liturgies and various activities. The post offered exactly the kind of stability I was looking for. In Liverpool I would have the time to focus on the inner healing I felt I needed.

Spiritual growth is a lifelong process, I have learned, as is healing the wounds of childhood or adulthood. In order to get in touch with the child within me, I had one-to-one counselling with Father Herlihy and Father Grant. I had to learn to feel what I should have felt when I was a kid: the anger, pain, rejection and loneliness.

During those three months of counselling, I began to experience a real sense of freedom and healing. At times, I just cried my eyes out. I felt I was, in a sense, returning home. Alongside the counselling, I spent hours in front of the Blessed Sacrament, asking Jesus to help me meet the child within, the child who was locked up. We all lock up things inside us that we don't want to face. There are key experiences in our childhood that determine the kind of person we become. The time when I didn't see my mum for six months emerged as one of the most significant moments in my childhood.

One day, when I was praying, I had an image of me showing a picture to Mum and Dad and both of them telling me to clear off. I didn't really understand what the meaning of this was. Later, I decided to phone Father Justin to tell him what I'd done that day. I then realised how much I needed affirmation from other people, because I hadn't received it as a child. That need for affirmation, I believe, was one of the main reasons why having an underworld reputation was so important for me. I can see now that I needed to be affirmed by people such as Bulldog, Jim, Phil and Syed. They saw me as someone important and special. Today, I no longer beat myself up over this need for affirmation. I've learned to be more compassionate with myself.

There are parts of our personality which we can't change

without the help of God. This isn't easy, however, as some areas of our life are very dark and scary. I'm still having counselling today, because I believe that spiritual growth and inner healing are lifelong processes. Prayer is the key. I take full responsibility for the choices I've made in my life. I don't blame anyone else. I leave the past to the mercy of God, the future to the providence of God, and the present to the love of God.

When I came down to lunch one day at St Austin's, Father David said, 'We could have done with you a few minutes ago.'

'Why?' I asked. 'What happened?'

'We found a man trying to break in. But he ran off when he was disturbed. Father Gerald has gone after him.'

'I'd better give him a hand,' I replied. A couple of weeks before, someone had broken into the presbytery and stolen a laptop computer. It was probably the same bloke, I thought.

I ran down the street to where Father Gerald was leaning against a wall, out of breath. 'He went that way, John,' he wheezed.

I ran as fast as I could, and then ahead of me I saw a stocky character running at a trot. Although I wasn't as fit as I used to be when I was doing the doors, I soon caught up with him and grabbed his shoulder.

'I'm making a citizen's arrest,' I said, wrestling him to the ground and placing my knee across his chest. 'Why are you breaking into churches?'

'Let me go! I need the money for drugs.' The guy squirmed, struggling to get free.

'They'll never fulfil you, mate.'

'How do you know?'

I looked down at him. He was in his mid-twenties and had what I can only describe as a dead look in his eyes. I didn't feel anger towards him, only compassion. Before I could answer his question, however, a police van pulled up. Two officers jumped out, knelt down, handcuffed the bloke and put him in the back of the van.

'Well done,' said one of the officers to me. 'It's a shame there aren't more people like you.'

I nodded. If only you knew, mate, I thought to myself.

As I watched the police van speed off into the distance, I said a prayer for the bloke inside, thinking, there but for the grace of God go I.

Fourteen

The proposal

'S TACEY?'
    'What is it, John?'

'You make me want to be a better person,' I said and then added hesitantly, 'Will you marry me? I want to spend the rest of my life with you.' I could hear the strains of a country and western song playing in the background.

She leant across the table towards me, smiled, and said, 'Yes, John.'

'You will?' I said, clasping her hand.

She nodded. The tears were streaming down her face. 'I think God is really calling us to be one.'

I slipped off the gold ring which had belonged to my step-father and put it on to her finger. As I did this, I saw out of the corner of my eye that one of the waitresses was dabbing her eyes with a hanky.

I was sitting with Stacey in Applejacks, a steak house on the way to Hartsfield International Airport in Atlanta. I'd just spent two and a half weeks in Marietta, a small city in the southern state of Georgia. The last thing I'd expected was that I'd end up falling in love.

Father Justin had suggested I go to Marietta to observe how Life Teen operated. He figured that a visit there might make me more enthusiastic about the programme being set up in St Austin's. I hadn't really wanted to go, but I did.

I was now leading a community of eight in St Austin's. Apart from myself there was Declan, who I'd first met at New Dawn in Walsingham four years previously; his brother Peter; Raphael, from Germany; Beth, who had been involved in

Youth 2000 for a few years and was thinking about joining the Franciscan Sisters of the Renewal in New York; Adam, who was into acting and music; Paul, a Scouser, who felt that he might have a vocation to the priesthood; and Todd, an American in his early twenties who had been invited over by Father Justin to set up the Life Teen programme.

We'd moved into The White House, two four-bedroom houses that had been knocked into one, on the opposite side of the car park from the church and presbytery. The guys lived in one part of the house and the girls in the other. Apart from Todd and myself, everyone was either studying at university or had jobs. But they had all made a commitment to live in community.

I'd never run a community before and I hadn't found it easy. I'd had to learn the difficult lesson that you can't control people and that you have to allow them to make mistakes. At the meetings we held every Monday I often had to remind everyone that they needed to stick to the rota for cleaning and washing up. 'We don't just need to pray together but we also need to keep the house clean,' I would say.

'John, I think it would be a good idea if you were to go out to Life Teen in the US and see how they do things,' Father Justin had suggested one morning in the presbytery after Mass.

'You think so, Father?' I replied with little enthusiasm in my voice. I hadn't been that impressed with Todd's ideas.

'Yes, I think it would help,' he replied.

'Okay,' I shrugged. 'If you really think it will make a difference, I'll go.'

To me, the Life Teen approach to faith and spirituality seemed too frothy. It lacked the substance and teaching I'd found in Youth 2000. For example, prayer wasn't as important as I felt it should be and adoration of the Blessed Sacrament was missing from the programme. What's more, I'd been told not to encourage the kids to go to confession.

Todd and I had increasingly begun to clash over the way

the programme should be run and this was affecting the community life. Both Todd and Father Justin felt that Life Teen should be very professional in its approach. I agreed with this, so long as it was Spirit-led. Not the other way around.

'The problem with Youth 2000, John,' Todd said to me one day in the kitchen, 'is that it's a pre-Vatican II type of Catholicism. Young people today don't want this. You need to have a more modern approach.'

'Listen, Todd, Youth 2000 promotes the teachings of the Church,' I replied, feeling my anger rising. 'It focuses on the Mass, confession, adoration and prayer. So you're telling me that's pre-Vatican II?'

'I think it's too rigid,' he retorted.

'What's rigid about it?'

'You don't need to pray at fixed times. You should pray when you feel like praying. I can pray when I'm sitting alone in my room strumming my guitar.' Todd wouldn't join the rest of the community when we met each morning for an hour's prayer in the small oratory.

I tried to stay calm. 'I understand what you're saying, Todd, but I think it's important that we have discipline in our prayer life.' This was one of the valuable lessons I'd taken away from my time with the Franciscan Friars of the Renewal.

Todd didn't really understand what Youth 2000 was about and the incredible impact it had had on thousands of young people. And I could see that, as an American, he didn't understand the Catholic culture in England. The kids here were used to more low-key liturgies rather than the ones he had been used to in the US. He was young and keen, but he didn't have a great experience of life. I didn't dislike him. It was just that I didn't agree with his views.

Feeling unenthusiastic about the two and a half weeks that lay ahead of me in Marietta, I heaved my black holdall bag off the baggage carousel at Hartsfield International Airport and made my way through the crowds to the arrivals lounge. Scanning the faces standing behind the barrier, I soon recognised Linda, who I'd met at World Youth Day in Rome in 2000.

'Hi, John, good to see you again,' she said brightly, and led me out of the airport terminal to the car park.

We left the airport behind and were soon driving past the high-rise blocks of bustling, downtown Atlanta. But it wasn't long before we were in the middle of some beautiful, rolling countryside, decked with flowers.

We arrived at a presbytery next to a large, modern church with steps leading up to it. It had been arranged for me to spend my first couple of nights here and then stay with a local family for the remainder of the visit.

A friendly looking priest in an unbuttoned Bermuda-type shirt and matching shorts greeted me at the door and showed me to my room. It was large and with an en-suite bathroom.

After I'd unpacked, I came downstairs and found the priest sprawled in an armchair in the living room watching baseball on a massive TV.

'Father, is there an oratory here?' I asked.

He looked up and said, 'No, I ripped it out to put a jacuzzi in.'

I laughed at his joke and waited for him to tell me where the oratory was.

'No. I did. We have a lovely jacuzzi now. You're welcome to use it.'

I told him politely that I'd pass on the jacuzzi, if it was all right with him, and go into the church to pray instead. I was glad I was only spending two nights here. It wasn't my kind of presbytery.

The next morning after Mass, I went to the Life Teen office, which was situated beneath the church. One part of it was the international Life Teen headquarters and the other part the local Life Teen centre. Apart from offices, there was also a room with pool and table tennis tables.

I was introduced to Chris, a sporty-looking guy in his late twenties who was the youth minister of the church, and Randy, the international director of Life Teen. In his late forties, he was married with seven children.

'I hear you pray the rosary,' Randy said with a broad smile, as he showed my around the offices.

'That's right.'

'That's great, John. The rosary's a powerful prayer.'

I knew when he said this that he had a love for Our Lady, and I warmed to him immediately.

He then said, 'Tell me, what do you think of Todd?'

'I think he's a nice guy and that he has a lot of courage in coming to England to run a Life Teen programme.'

'But what do you really think of him?'

'I'm not going to bad-mouth him. I don't like to gossip.' I wondered if Randy was testing me.

The following morning at the Life Teen international office I was introduced to an attractive, slim woman in her early twenties with long shoulder-length brown hair. She told me her name was Stacey and that she was originally from New York.

'What do you plan to do eventually?' she asked with interest.

'I might become a priest,' I replied. I had been to see the vocations director in the Liverpool diocese, although I still wasn't sure if God was calling me to priesthood. But I decided to keep the door open.

'Really?'

'Yeah, if I think that's what God is calling me to do.' I then told her about my time with the friars in New York and that I now ran a community in Liverpool.

'So how do you earn your money?'

'I live off God's providence,' I answered.

She looked surprised. 'You do?'

I nodded. 'I place my trust in Jesus.' Then grinning, I added, 'He hasn't let me down yet.'

She then invited me to an American football match the next day.

'Well, I don't know anything about American football,' I said.

She laughed. 'Don't worry. I'll teach you.'

The following morning, Stacey, accompanied by her two teenage sisters, picked me up in her blue Jeep from the house of the family I was now staying with, and we set off for the Georgia Tech football stadium in Atlanta. It was packed. There must have been about 20,000 people there. Although I didn't really understand the rules, despite Stacey excitedly explaining them to me, I still found the game interesting – and the hot dogs with chilli were great!

Afterwards, we went back to her mum's house for lunch. During the meal, Stacey asked if I wanted to go to adoration with her at a church in a small town just outside Marietta. I immediately said yes, as there was no adoration at the church run by the priest in the Bermuda-style shirt. We started doing this each evening. After leaving the church, we'd stop off at a twenty-four-hour waffle house in a shopping mall, where we'd chat over a coffee until, sometimes, the early hours of the morning.

We often prayed the rosary as we drove along. One evening, on our way to the waffle house, I began singing Beautiful Lady, a hymn to Our Lady. I noticed that Stacey was crying at the end of it.

'Is my singing that bad?' I chuckled.

'No, John,' she said, shaking her head. 'That hymn really touched me.'

I started to find myself being attracted to Stacey. We both opened up to each other about our lives. I felt I could talk to her about anything. Although she was twenty-three and I was thirty-six, she was very mature. I was committed to living as a single lay man and, if it was God's will, going to seminary at some point in the future. But my feelings for Stacey started to grow as I spent more time with her and she told me about herself. I was very impressed when she revealed that she'd undertaken a pro-life walk all the way from Atlanta to Washington. She also admitted that she'd been in some bad relationships, and had been hurt, before finding God. I started to pray about my relationship with her.

I have always loved playing pool, so It was great to be able to have a few games with Chris – and to take him to the cleaners.

'I thought Americans were meant to be the best at pool,' he joked after I beat him for the umpteenth time.

'Well, you might have invented it, but we know how to play it,' I laughed. 'You know what they say in England, Chris?'

'What?'

'Pool is the sign of a misspent youth.'

'You know, John, you seem to give God everything, even though, like me, you're broken. I mean, I've always believed in God but I feel that I've never been able to give him everything.'

'Do you pray much?' I asked.

'Yeah and I go to Mass every day.'

'Well, why don't you do a holy hour each day. There's great grace in it.'

'Yeah?'

'There's great healing in making a holy hour. You can't sit under the sun without receiving a suntan and in the same way you can't sit in the presence of God without receiving his love deep within your heart.'

One evening, I felt God asking me to pray over him. But I didn't want him to feel awkward, so I asked him to pray over me first.

'Sure, John,' he said.

We went into the church and sat in a dark side chapel. As Chris prayed over me, I felt that my childhood wounds were being healed. I could see an image of Jesus on the cross and me as a child. I picked up this child, kissed him and walked over to the cross, where we both kissed the crucified Christ. As I embraced the child, I felt that, through the sufferings of

Christ on the cross, I was made whole and that I was free within myself.

'That was amazing,' I said to Chris, fighting back the tears, and I told him about the picture I'd seen in my heart.

He squeezed my shoulder and said, 'I can see that you've received a great healing.'

Early one sunny morning, under a clear blue sky, I went with Chris and Randy in a Land Rover on a six-hour drive down to the Florida coast to have lunch with Dwight, a wealthy businessman. Randy explained that he'd not only given generously to Life Teen, but had also paid for his local church to be built, in honour of his son, who had died, and for numerous young people to work in Mexico as missionaries.

On the way, we stopped off at a petrol station in a small town. Noticing a group of black guys sitting on the steps of a house, drinking beer, I got out of the Land Rover and walked across the road to them.

'How are you doing?' I asked cheerily.

'Where are you from with that accent, man?' said a guy in a red baseball cap, taking a sip from his can.

'London,' I smiled.

'Boy, that's one great accent you got there.'

I then took out several Miraculous Medals from my pocket and handed one to each of them.

'What are they?' asked the man with the red baseball cap, looking intrigued.

I explained how the medals had been made after St Catherine Laboure had experienced visions of Our Lady in 1830 at a convent in Paris. 'They were made so that each person might know how loved they are by Mary,' I explained.

'That's beautiful, man. I believe in Jesus. Now I know that his mother will be praying for me as well,' he said, placing the medal around his neck.

'God bless you,' I said, turning to walk back to the Land Rover, and then added, 'And don't drink too much.'

They all laughed and the guy in the red baseball cap called out, 'Respect, man!'

It turned out that the businessman lived in a huge mansion whose grounds extended all the way down to the sea. A number of large, expensive-looking cars were parked along the drive. We joined about forty other people, mainly business leaders, lawyers, doctors and politicians, for a fabulous four-course meal. When I went out on to the balcony for a ciggy, he came out to chat to me. I was impressed that he took time out to talk to me with so many important guests to entertain.

After the meal, Chris and I went for a stroll along the beach and I asked him if he was going to marry Kerry, his girlfriend. I'd met her the day before at the Life Teen office and had thought that she was very beautiful.

'No,' he replied a little sheepishly. 'I don't think I love her enough.'

'So why are you going out with her?'

'What do you mean?'

'Well, why are you going out with her if you don't love her enough to get married to her?'

He pursed his lips and nodded. 'You're right, John, I shouldn't be going out with her.'

Chris took me into a local high school one morning to talk to some of the kids and invite them to a Life Teen night the following Sunday, where I was due to give a talk. Walking through the school gates, I felt a bit nervous, as I hadn't done this sort of thing for quite a while. Chris and I chatted with some of the kids in the dining room over lunch, but I thought they seemed more fascinated by my accent than by what I was saying.

But there was one girl who, I could tell, was deeply wounded. She was dressed in the Goth style of all black and she had an upside-down cross hanging around her neck.

I went and sat down next to her and started telling her about God's love for her. But she just mocked me and told me to get a life.

A few days later, Stacey and I were sitting in a coffee shop when the girl walked in with some friends, all of them dressed in black. When I went over to her and invited her to the Life Teen night, she replied with a bored look, 'Well, I'll be there in spirit.'

'John, you know I feel a real heaviness here for some reason,' Stacey said when I went back to the table.

'Don't worry, Stacey. I've had this before.'

'What do you mean?'

'It's people praying against us. I know from experience that a lot of kids get involved in this sort of stuff, dressing up as Goths, listening to heavy death music and playing with the Ouija board, and they think it's a laugh. But they can get seriously hurt by it. I know kids that are in mental hospitals in England because of this.'

Around two hundred teenagers, including some from the school, turned up at the church for the Life Teen night on Sunday. The Mass was accompanied by lively music, the priest – from another parish – gave a powerful homily and the teenagers went up on to the sanctuary and gathered around the altar. Following Mass, in a room off the church, I told my life story and encouraged the kids to pray and go to confession.

The reactions of the kids to what I said, particularly about the hurt I had experienced in my childhood, and the time I had spent in prayer since I'd been in Marietta, made me feel that God was telling me to evangelise when I returned to Liverpool. The joy I'd previously experienced when I'd evangelised with Youth 2000 had returned.

The next morning, Stacey and I drove to a Trappist monastery, an hour or so from Marietta. In the cool, light church we prayed over each other and for each other. Kneeling there with Stacey, I felt that God was calling us to be together. My thoughts about priesthood seemed to have disappeared.

'Stacey, I can see a picture of Our Lady with her arms around us,' I said.

182

She turned to me and said softly, 'That's beautiful.'

Arriving back in Liverpool, I was not only in love with Stacey but also on fire with the desire to evangelise. My visit to Life Teen had been more inspirational than I could ever have imagined, as a result of meeting Randy and Chris.

I told Father Justin that I felt God was calling me to evangelise in schools, not just in the parish.

'Well, we need to pray about this,' he said.

'Father, this is something I've prayed about already and this is what I believe God is calling me to do,' I replied, feeling that he was pouring cold water over what I said.

'I'm not so sure.'

'Why? Is it because of the retreat we had at the school that time?' We'd run a retreat in a local school and it had been a disaster. A lot of the kids hadn't been that interested and in the early hours of the morning some of them had started running around the school and causing mayhem. I'd had to get out of bed, drive to the school and take four of them back to their parents.

'Your job is here in St Austin's, John.'

'So how do we attract kids if there's no contact with schools?'

'Okay,' he said with reluctance. 'If that's what you think.' But I could see that he didn't seem convinced by what I'd said.

The next day, I began phoning secondary schools in the city and arranging for myself and some of the community to go in to give talks or lead a retreat. We then started holding Life Teen nights after the Sunday evening Mass. Kids soon started coming along in increasing numbers. But I soon got disappointed by the nights as I felt they were quite superficial. There wasn't enough solid teaching. I felt that these nights didn't have as much depth as the nights I had seen in Marietta. But it was clear that Todd was determined to run things his way.

One of the things I have learned in my spiritual journey is that you can only pass on what you've got. So if you only have a shallow faith, then you can't lead others to a deep faith. And I felt that Todd's faith, unlike that of Chris, wasn't strong enough yet to lead young people to a deeper relationship with Jesus. The Life Teen programme depends so much on who is running it, whereas Youth 2000 doesn't, because its focus is the sacraments, which never change.

In December, I was glad of the opportunity to leave Liverpool and travel to Dublin to lead a Youth 2000 retreat at Esker Retreat House, run by the Redemptorists, in Athenry, County Galway. I took the blue Saab 9000 car, generously given to me by Tony Standish, a Liverpool car dealer. I'd met him in a hotel in Lourdes when I'd gone there with the St Austin's parish pilgrimage in the summer. I'd been asked to give a talk and encourage young people to get more involved in leadership in Youth 2000. I hadn't been involved with Youth 2000 since the retreat at Liverpool Cathedral on New Year's Eve 1999.

Therese Devaney, the national leader of Youth 2000 in Ireland, said to me one afternoon after we came out of the chapel, 'What can we do to really break Youth 2000 open and make it more vibrant? I want it to reach more young people. A lot of those who come to retreats are the same people.'

'One of the things is to break Ireland into regions, like Youth 2000 has done in England, and have regional leaders you can trust setting up retreats,' I suggested.

'That's a good idea, I can see how it would work,' she said.

The retreat at Esker was powerful and I saw a lot of young people being changed and returning to the sacraments. I went back to Liverpool fired up with my faith.

Stacey came over just before Christmas to stay with me for a couple of weeks. She told me that Todd had been slagging me off to Randy, Chris, and other people in Life Teen.

'You need to defend yourself,' she urged.

'Why do I need to defend myself? God knows the truth,' I

replied, lighting a cigarette. I saw no point in getting into a slanging match with Todd.

I agreed to help with a Life Teen event on New Year's Eve at St Austin's. A few days before, I drove with Stacey along icy roads to Harrogate in North Yorkshire to take part in a Youth 2000 retreat at St John Fisher School.

When I arrived, I was told that I was to be the MC. As it had been over a year since I'd acted as MC, I asked Neil and Sister Miriana, who had both travelled there from the Community of the Beatitudes in France, to pray over me in one of the empty classrooms.

'John, there's something I feel God wants me to say to you,' said Neil.

'What is it?'

'Don't keep on asking God to use you, John. Know that he is using you,' he told me.

When he said this, it really hit me that so many times I'd asked God to use me instead of trusting that he was already doing so.

Father John Edwards, whom I'd met at Allington Castle some years before, was also at the retreat.

'Father John, do you remember that you once said to me that I was going to be a leader and that God would use me to bring thousands of souls to him?'

He grinned. 'Yes.'

'Well, I thought you were off your head at the time, but lots of things have happened since then.' I then told him what had taken place in my life since we had met. 'It proves, Father, that God can use anyone, even someone as broken as me.'

Because the snow was so heavy, the roads out of Harrogate were unpassable, and I was unable to get back to Liverpool for the Life Teen night. When I phoned Father Justin to tell him that I wouldn't be able to make it, he wasn't too pleased and told me to get my priorities right.

The conversation with Father Justin was still on my mind when I attended the healing service in the school hall that night. But when the priest carrying the Blessed Sacrament stopped in front of me, I felt Jesus say to me that Youth 2000 was my priority. It was a moment of revelation. I knew that I was going to leave St Austin's, even though I had security in Liverpool. I had my own room, food, a car, and a phone. Could I give this up? How would I survive? I had to trust in God. Even though God had provided for me when I'd left the Kingsmead Estate for the Family House of Prayer in Scotland, I realised that I still had a lack of trust in him.

When I got back to St Austin's I told Father Justin of my decision. I wasn't sure how he'd react.

He gave me a hug. 'We're all going to miss you, John. We've had our differences, but that's normal.'

I'd received much healing while at St Austin's. Father Justin and I had very different spiritualities. But through his patience, love and tolerance, he'd supported me and allowed me to grow. And I was grateful to him for that. I knew that, at times, I probably hadn't been easy to live with.

One cold, wet afternoon in early February, I packed away my clothes, breviary and Bible into my holdall bag, put it in the back of the Saab and drove to Harrogate to stay with Father Richard Aladics for a few days. I wanted to get his advice and also pray about what God wanted me to do – also, Father Richard was a brilliant cook, so I knew that I'd eat well while I was there.

'What do you think I should do, Father?' I asked as we sat in his living room that night after a delicious paella.

He thought for a moment. 'I've always seen you as an evangelist, John. I think that's what you should be doing. That is your gift.'

'This confirms what I feel God has been saying to me, Father.'

The following morning, I drove the short distance to East Keswick in Leeds to see Robert Toone, the national leader of Youth 2000. He had phoned me the night before and invited me to his house for a chat.

Robert and I talked about what I might do and then he said, 'John, do you fancy running the mission team and going on the road?'

My eyes lit up. The time Neil and I had spent on the road with Youth 2000 had been brilliant. 'Well, I would if I can just be on the road. That's where I feel God is calling me. I don't really want to spend a lot of my time in community because I've had enough of it in Liverpool.'

We agreed that I'd join Youth 2000 in March. The plan was that I'd do three weeks on the road and then take one week off. Josie Callaghan, who had turned her back on a high-flying career as a scientist to work for Youth 2000, would be in charge of running things from the office but I'd be in charge of the mission team on the road. This seemed ideal.

Driving back to Harrogate through the beautiful Yorkshire countryside, I saw a marvellous rainbow in the sky. Transfixed, I stopped the car, got out and stood by the roadside staring up at it. I felt that I'd made the right decision in leaving Liverpool and rejoining Youth 2000. In the Bible, the rainbow was a sign from God to Noah that he wouldn't flood the earth again. The rainbow to me had always been a sign from God that this was where he wanted me to be.

A few days later, I flew to Dublin to work with Youth 2000 Ireland for a month. Paul Rooney, who had been made regional leader for Dublin, had invited me to come over after the week I'd spent in Ireland before Christmas.

I stayed with Father Adrian Crowley at The Holy Family Church in Aughrim Street, a busy parish in a working-class district of the city, just north of the River Liffey.

He gave me a warm welcome and told me my room was upstairs.

'Peace be to you and your house, Father,' I said, as I started to climb the stairs. I was halfway up when my feet suddenly went from under me as the staircase collapsed, leaving me clinging onto the banisters with my feet dangling.

Seeing that I was okay, Father Adrian burst out laughing.

'Peace be to my house? You've only been here a few minutes and you've caused mayhem.'

One Friday evening, Father Adrian drove me to the Morning Star and Regina Caeli hostels in Brunswick Street. On the way, he explained that this was where Frank Duff had founded the Legion of Mary in 1921, and added that we'd also be able to visit his house, which had been preserved as a museum.

When I walked into the Regina Caeli hostel, my eyes latched on to a picture hanging on the wall. It was of Jesus with his arms wide open. Crowding around him were beggars, prostitutes, crippled children and all sorts of broken people. As I looked at the picture, I felt the Holy Spirit go through me and that this was what I wanted to be doing: bringing broken people like this to the body of Christ. And I felt an incredible closeness to Our Lady.

When Father Adrian and I got back to the presbytery shortly before midnight, he said, 'I want to show you something.'

He led me into the church and we both knelt down. Looking at the flickering sanctuary lamp, I felt such grace and power from God. I turned to him and said, 'Why is there so much power coming out from the tabernacle?'

'What night is it?' he asked.

'Friday,' I replied.

'And what's everyone up to?'

I knew what he meant. Many people would be out getting drunk in pubs nightclubs and sleeping around, as I had once done, oblivious to the fact that the grace and mercy of God was pouring out from the tabernacle. I felt God say to me that I could ask him anything. So I asked for the grace to give up smoking and become a saint – although I wasn't sure which would be the hardest.

'I'm going to tell you a story,' said Father Adrian, sitting down. 'There were two curates who were being badly treated by the parish priest. So they decided to leave. Early one morning they packed their bags and crept out of the presbytery and into the church, which was the only way out to the street. As they were walking down the aisle, one of them said to the other, "Let's just kneel and say a prayer." So they knelt down. After about an hour, one of them said, "I can't leave him." And the other said, "I can't leave either." They could have left the priest, but they couldn't leave Jesus in the Blessed Sacrament.'

'That's a lovely story, Father. Tell me, why do you pray so much?' I'd never met anyone who prayed as much as Father Adrian.

'When I pray I'm a nice person; when I don't pray I'm horrible,' he replied, adding that he often found it difficult to forgive people who had hurt him.

I learned that during a three-year period he'd knocked on the door of every person who lived in the parish and spent at least half an hour with anyone who invited him in.

Father Adrian had said that he'd phone the chaplain at Mountjoy Prison in Dublin to see if it could be arranged for me to give a talk to some of the inmates. While we were spending a couple of days with his brother in Cork, I asked him if he'd rung the chaplain yet.

'Not yet,' he replied.

I said, 'Think of all the souls that could be lost.' And I knew instantly that what I'd said was stupid.

I travelled back to Dublin ahead of Father Adrian, as I was taking part in a retreat in the south of the city. When he came back the next evening he didn't look very happy.

'Father, are you all right?' I asked when he walked into the living room.

'No, not really,' he said.

'Do you want to talk about it?'

'Not at the moment,' he replied sullenly. 'I'll talk about it in the morning.'

I figured that someone had upset him.

The next morning at breakfast I said, 'So who upset you, Father?

'It was you.'

'Me?' I was taken aback.

'Yes, you really hurt me when you said about all those souls being lost.'

'Look, Father, I'm very sorry. It was a stupid thing to say and I should have apologised immediately. I'm such an idiot. It was one of those spur of the moment things. I'm humbly sorry.'

He looked hard at me and then said slowly, 'Do you know what, John, I feel so much grace from this, because I've never been able to speak like this. I've not spoken to people for years from seminary because they hurt me. It seems like God has enabled me to do this with you rather than bottle it up.

Forgiveness, I have discovered both from my own life and people I've spoken to, is a major issue. Yet if we don't forgive each other, how can we expect to be forgiven? Our lack of forgiveness often prevents us from being truly free and healed.

During the month, I helped out at a number of retreats in and around Dublin and Sligo. One Sunday, I preached at all the Masses at St Mary's Cathedral in Sligo at the invitation of the bishop. Walking through the town afterwards, people kept coming up to talk to me in the street and asking, 'Are you the gangster?'. I smiled back and said, 'I'm only a gangster for God now.' This is what it must be like for David Beckham, I thought to myself each time I shook another hand.

At a retreat at a school in Dublin, a young woman came up to me and said that she'd been taking drugs and sleeping around.

'I didn't really want to come here, but a friend persuaded me. I'm so glad that I did though,' she said.

'Why?' I asked, feeling that I knew the answer already.

'Because I've been to confession for the first time in years and I now feel that I have God in my life. I only took the drugs and slept around because I hated myself. I was very unhappy.'

I said to her, 'Every time you look in the mirror I want you to say to yourself that you are beautiful and loved by God.'

Stacey and her friend Christine, who was about to enter a Poor Clare convent in Alabama, came to Ireland to spend a couple of weeks with me. But I saw very little of them as I was so busy with talks and retreats. I felt quite guilty about this.

My month in Ireland had been brilliant. I was delighted to be asked to lead two Youth 2000 retreats, one in Newry and one near Dublin, in October. On the night before I left, I said to Father Adrian, 'I need to tell you something, Father.'

'What's that?'

'Look, Father, I've learned so much from you. You've taught me so much about myself and my weaknesses. And I just want to say . . .'

'Stop!' he interrupted, moving swiftly towards the door, and then looking back, grinned, 'If you want to tell me that I'm a worm and a nasty horrible person, then I'll stay up. But if you're going to flatter me, then I'm going to bed.' And he did.

Before Stacey had returned to America, she had told me that she wanted to spend six months with the Youth 2000 mission team in England so that she could be with me. After her two weeks with me in Ireland, I was now having second thoughts about getting married, as I wasn't sure I loved her enough. I remembered what I had said to Chris about his relationship with his girlfriend that time we walked along the beach in Florida. My heart seemed to be more in evangelis-ation than in a relationship. So I went to see Father Pat Deegan, one of my spiritual directors, at the Family House of Prayer in Scotland.

He said, 'You should ask her to come.'

'I should?'

He nodded. 'Yes, because after six months you'll know whether to marry her or not.'

That night, I phoned Stacey and told her to come to England. She was over the moon.

When I drove to East Keswick to begin my work with the Youth 2000 mission team, I felt a very different person to what I'd been in Liverpool. The month in Ireland had really fired me up with wanting to bring Jesus to young people – and I'd also managed to quit smoking.

The mission team consisted of Declan and Paul, who had both lived with me in Liverpool and three girls, two of whom were called Catherine. Catherine V who had drifted away from God in her teens and then come back. Catherine U, a very gentle girl, who had been home-schooled by her parents and was going on to be a doctor; and Emilia, who was planning to go to Cambridge University to study law.

The plan was that I'd travel with either three or two of the team at any one time for a week and we'd stay overnight in presbyteries, convents and religious houses. The remaining members of the team would help out Josie in the office.

Our first time on the road was on the south coast in Brighton, where we were to lead a weekend retreat in a school. We all went there, along with Josie. The Friday night turned out to be quite difficult, as a lot of the kids didn't seem that interested. Josie then suggested that I gave a talk about how I'd found God.

Afterwards, four tough-looking young lads came up to me when I was having a cup of coffee. 'Was all that true?' asked one of them.

'Yeah. It was.'

'Did you ever go to these sort of things?'

'I was converted at one of them.'

'Yeah?'

'Yeah. Now listen very carefully,' I began. 'If you go to confession at this retreat, and you're honest, at the healing service tomorrow night when Jesus comes round you will know that he's real. And I bet that you'll feel better than if I gave you a cheque for a million quid.'

They didn't look very convinced when I said this. But the following night after the healing service the four of them came up to me, beaming. They all said that they had done as I said and they felt fantastic – but they probably would still have liked the cheque for a million quid.

Declan, Emilia and I then travelled to Lewisham, in south-east London, to run a retreat. I realised that I was becoming more and more irritable with them as the week went on. When they returned to East Keswick they told Josie and Robert that they didn't want to go on the road with me again because I'd treated them badly.

Robert asked to have a chat with me. He told me that Declan and Emilia felt very hurt. I apologised and told him that it wouldn't happen again. I saw that I'd put the work before them and had overlooked the fact that they'd never been on the road before. Like me, they were broken. What they really needed was love and affirmation. While I was good at challenging people, I was not so good at affirming them. And I realised that it was only through loving each other that we could love the kids we met.

When the two Catherines and Paul came with me the following week to run a retreat in Bristol, I made sure that I built them up and didn't repeat the mistakes I'd made with Declan and Emilia.

I had mixed feelings when Stacey left Marietta and came to East Keswick to begin working with Youth 2000 in the office. It wasn't long before I began to feel guilty again that I wasn't spending enough time with her. I was always out on the road running retreats.

'When are you going to spend some time with me? Aren't I important to you?' she said to me one day.

'It's very difficult, Stacey,' I said. 'I don't have any time at the moment.' Yet I realised that when she'd come over to

Liverpool and Ireland I hadn't spent much time with her, even when I had a day off.

During a retreat in Darlington I asked Catherine U what she was going to do when her six months with the mission team ended.

'I'm going to medical school in London,' she answered.

'Why?' She didn't seem that enthusiastic.

'Because lots of people are expecting me to be a doctor.'

'You don't live your life for other people. You live it for God.' I replied.

She looked at me thoughtfully and said, 'I hadn't looked at it that way before.'

Stacey travelled with me up to Scotland, where I was to MC a retreat at the Family House of Prayer. Throughout the journey, I sensed that she wasn't very happy.

'John, I'm your fiancée but we hardly ever spend any time together. You're running around doing all this good work. But when are you going to spend some time with me?'

I found myself thinking that she was being very clingy. 'Well, Stacey, that's the way it is at the moment. I'm sorry, Stacey,' I replied sharply.

After a few days there, we travelled to the Community of the Beatitudes in France. The community, which consisted of priests, religious, single lay people and married couples, lived in a rambling old house in the Normandy countryside. But even there I didn't spend enough time with Stacey. And I'd taken up smoking again.

Sister Mirjana prayed over me in the chapel one evening. 'I feel there are still areas in your life where you need healing about the violence in both your childhood and adulthood, John,' she said. She had revealed that before joining the community, she had been involved with the Hells Angels when she was younger.

She was right. I was aware that, at times, I could lose my temper very easily, and I didn't feel as free as I knew Jesus wanted me to be.

194

On the ferry coming back to England, I stood on the deck staring out across the choppy sea, with a sharp wind blowing on my face, wondering what I should do with my life. Should I go to America, get married and become a youth minister in a parish, as Stacey wanted me to do? Or should I continue living as a single man relying on God's providence?

Over the next few weeks, I prayed about this. As the schools had closed for the summer, I had a lot of time on my hands. So I went to London to see my mum and dad. Each day, I asked God to give me guidance about my future. I saw little of Stacey during this period, as she was busy helping to organise the conference in Walsingham.

In early August I drove to a retreat centre in the Wirral to lead a confirmation programme. It went brilliantly. Seeing how many kids went to confession really touched me. One lad came up to me and said that although he'd gone to Mass with his parents he hadn't really understood until now that he was loved by Jesus.

After the confirmation programme had finished, I sat in the car and prayed, 'Look, God, I've been asking you for a month to give me an answer about what I should do with my life. And you haven't done it. You know how much I love evangelising. Please give me an answer.' I then turned the ignition key, put on a tape called Revival in Belfast by Robin Mark, which Emilia had left in my car, and headed back to East Keswick. As I waited for a set of traffic lights to change, I heard the words of the song: 'When it's all been said and done/There's just one thing that matters/Did you live your life for me?/Did you live your life for the truth?' I then remembered Callum at the Family House of Prayer once saying that the most important thing in life was to bring as many souls to God as possible and our own first. I knew that the answer to my prayer was that I should evangelise.

At the New Dawn Conference in Walsingham I asked Neil and John McKenna, a friend who was training for the priesthood at Allen Hall seminary in London, what they both thought I should do with my life. They told me that I should evangelise.

God speaks to us through other people. And he doesn't just speak once he speaks time and time again. He had used Father Richard, Callum, Neil, and John to tell me that he wanted me to evangelise.

Stacey and I travelled to Bideford, a pretty town on the Devon coast, to spend a week with Father John Bielawski, who had offered to give us both spiritual direction and also arranged for me to give some talks in his parish.

'There's something I have to tell you,' I said to her as we walked along the quayside one afternoon.

She looked anxious. 'What is it, John?'

'I feel called to go and work in Ireland when my six months with the mission team ends.' I knew that if I didn't make this decision known I'd hurt her even more. She'd left her job, family and home to come to England just to be with me. And I'd hardly spent any time with her. I knew that there was a lot of work to be done in Ireland. After the month I'd spent there I'd been inundated with requests to help run retreats in schools and parishes.

'I feel called to America,' she said with sadness in her voice, then added brightly. 'So why don't you come over to America at Christmas? We can spend time together there.'

I shook my head. 'No, Stacey. You're going to America and I'm going to Ireland. I think that maybe God called us together to grow, but I don't think he's calling us to get married.' I felt very sad when I said this because I knew that she loved me deeply and also that she'd been hurt in some of her previous relationships. But I couldn't love her back in the same way, despite the fact that I'd always yearned for someone to really love me. But it wasn't enough.

Our six months as a community in East Keswick came to an end. On our last night we all had a meal together in the house. Each of us spoke about what had been the best times on the road.

'My best moment,' I said, 'was when each of you really gave your testimony from the heart.' I then recounted the places where I remembered them doing this well. 'It's also been great for me to see you all grow and change over these last six months. And I've learned a lot from you and I love you very much.'

The next morning, we all said our goodbyes and hugged each other. Each of us felt that the six months together had been a time of great spiritual growth. I then drove up with Catherine V and Paul to Scotland to lead a retreat on the Isle of Uist at the invitation of Father Roddy McCally.

I was sitting in the bar on the ferry having a drink when I glanced up at the TV and saw on Sky News the incredible sight of a plane flying into a tall building and then exploding in flames. I then saw people throwing themselves out of the windows. As I watched in shock, I learned that the World Trade Centre in New York had been attacked. I'd never seen anything like it. That night, I phoned Stacey, who was leaving for America the following day. She was in bits over the attack, as she had uncles and cousins in the New York fire service. I told her that all she could do was what Padre Pio had suggested: pray, hope and don't worry. And I said I'd also pray.

She phoned me the next day and told me that none of her family had been injured or killed in the attack, but colleagues of theirs had. She added that a number of those in the fire service had stopped off at the Franciscan Friars of the Renewal in the South Bronx and Harlem on their way to the World Trade Centre to receive conditional absolution in case they were killed in the carnage.

A few days before I left for Ireland, I phoned Stacey in Marietta. It was the Feast of St Therese of Lisieux, her favourite saint. We chatted for a while, but the conversation was a bit strained. 'I'll always be here for you and I'll always pray for you,' I said at the end.

'So will I,' she replied with emotion in her voice.

But when I put the phone down I decided not to contact

her again, as I felt I might hurt her more. She now needed to move on. God had brought us together, I believed, and we'd both received grace as a result of it. But he was now calling her to something else in America and he was calling me to work with Youth 2000 in Ireland. I didn't know what would happen after the two retreats there had finished. I was just putting my trust in God.

Fifteen

Bullets, brokenness and blessings

In October 2001 I left England for Ireland. Even though I believed it was God's will for me to go to Ireland, I felt a little unsure about it as I drove through North Wales to the ferry port at Holyhead. Youth 2000 in Ireland had paid for my ferry ticket and arranged accommodation for the two retreats I was to lead. But I didn't know what I'd do after that. All I had was my few possessions and a hundred quid in my wallet.

As I was sitting there in a long line of cars at Holyhead, waiting to be given the signal to drive onto the car ferry, my mobile phone rang.

'How are you, John?' It was Catherine U, who had been part of the Youth 2000 mission team.

'Hello, Catherine, I'm fine. I'm off to Ireland. What about you?'

'Well, I've something to tell you.' I could hear the excitement and emotion in her voice.

'What?'

'I'm entering Tyburn,' she said after a pause.

'You are? That's fantastic, Catherine!' I knew that Catherine was a very committed Catholic but this news took me by surprise. Tyburn was an enclosed Benedictine convent close to Marble Arch in London.

'I'm joining on the Feast of All Saints. And I'm going to pray for you every day, because it was while I was on the road with you that I received my vocation to the contemplative life.'

It was me who now started to feel emotional. I felt that God was telling me that I'd done my best in England and

FROM GANGLAND TO PROMISED LAND

that it was his will that I went to Ireland. 'You're always in my heart and in my prayers, Catherine,' I said.

When the ferry docked in Dublin, Padraig, whom I'd met during my month with Youth 2000 in Ireland, and also at the Family House of Prayer, was waiting for me. Despite having spina bifida, he worked full time in a company that made orthopaedic footwear.

'I'm going to take six months' leave of absence from work and I'm coming on the road with you,' he told me when we sat down for a meal that night at his house in the suburb of Blanchardstown in the west of the city.

'That's great, Padraig,' I said. I was thrilled to bits, as I felt that Padraig and I would be able to support each other.

The idea was that if Youth 2000 had arranged a retreat somewhere Padraig and I would spend the week beforehand going into schools, where I would give a talk and promote the retreat. And if there weren't any Youth 2000 retreats, I'd still give talks in schools or run one-day retreats, where we we'd have Mass, adoration and confession. When I'd been on the road in England, everything had been arranged for us by Josie in the Youth 2000 office. Padraig and I would now have to organise everything ourselves, like Neil and I had done that time.

Padraig and I then started visiting schools around Dublin to promote a retreat we were holding the following weekend in a retreat centre just outside the city. Around forty-five teenagers turned up. When I discovered that many of them had never been to a Youth 2000 event before, I was very pleased, as Youth 2000 in Ireland were keen to attract more new people.

I noticed that all the kids went to confession except one girl. I prayed that she might have the courage to do this. 'Jesus, if I can say anything that might help her, then let it happen.' That evening, I went out with a friend of mine to a Chinese restaurant for a meal. When I got back to the retreat centre, I went into the church to spend some time in adoration, which was going on throughout the night. After a while, I went into the centre for a cup of coffee. I saw the girl there, sitting with two friends.

'Can I have a word with you?' I said.

She looked startled for a moment. 'Yes,' she said, getting up and following me outside.

'I know the reason you didn't go to confession,' I said.

'No you don't. No one knows me. My boyfriend doesn't know me, nor does my dad or my mum. None of them know me,' she replied curtly.

'You're wrong. God knows you. And I can prove it. You didn't go to confession because you were sexually abused when you were younger,' I found myself saying.

She looked shocked when I said this and then burst out crying. After a while she said, 'How did you know?'

'I worked it out. You feel that you have to confess it and you're petrified to do so. But you don't have to confess it because it's not your sin. It was someone else's.' I felt that the Holy Spirit was telling me this.

She then went on to tell me how a family friend had abused her when she was ten years old. That night, I prayed that she would go to confession the next day. She did, and afterwards she came running down the corridor to where I was talking to someone and threw her arms around me.

'You were right, God does know me. And I've just met him.'

On Sunday afternoon, Padraig and I then drove north to Newry, just across the border, to promote a retreat the following weekend. On the way, I noticed that many houses were flying either Union Jacks or Irish tricolours. To me, this seemed very tribal and provocative, and it would do nothing to help the peace process, which was attempting to put an end to over thirty years of violence and killing in Northern Ireland.

We stayed at Dromantine Retreat and Conference Centre, a wonderful old house set in beautiful grounds at the end of a long drive. It was run by the Society of African Missions and had been a seminary at one time.

That evening at a prayer meeting, a middle-aged woman came up to us and asked if we'd pray over her. As we did, I felt that the Holy Spirit was telling me that she needed to be reconciled with her mother. When I told her this, she began sobbing.

'What's the matter?' I asked, sitting down next to her.

'I haven't spoken to my mother in years,' she admitted. 'I felt God saying that I should contact my mother. And now I will.'

At the end of the prayer meeting, a woman in her thirties came up to me and handed me her business card. She introduced herself as Eva and said if Padraig and I ever needed anything, we should phone her.

The reality of the troubles in Northern Ireland came home to me for the first time the next day when I met a guy who told me that his son refused to sleep in his bedroom at home because he'd looked out of his window one night and seen the IRA drag a guy out of the house across the street and shoot him in both knees. They'd claimed he was an informant. In fact, the man told me, he was a businessman who wouldn't pay them protection money.

My car needed its MOT done and its tax and insurance renewed, but we didn't have enough money. When I mentioned this to Padraig, he said, 'What about that woman in Newry who gave you her business card?'

So I phoned Eva and explained the situation. She said she was glad to be able to help and we met her the next day in a trendy restaurant on Lisburn Road in Belfast. She gave me enough money to cover the cost of the MOT, tax and the insurance. I was touched by her generosity. Over a meal, we then chatted about our respective spiritual journeys and struggles along the way. I encouraged her to go to confession and spend time in adoration. Two days later, she sent me a text message to say that she'd been to confession and now felt a tremendous pull to spend time with Jesus in the Blessed Sacrament. I thought to myself how true Jesus' words are that in giving we receive.

After a mission at St Teresa's Church, near Queen's University, Padraig and I went to run a retreat at St Peter's boys' school. During my talk, I spoke out against the violence of the paramilitaries.

A teenager came up to me after the talk and he said, 'You're allowed to use violence though to defend your country, aren't you?'

'Only in time of war,' I replied.

'Well, we are at war,' he came back at me.

'No, you're not. You can't use violence. It's wrong. You're not defending. You're attacking. And if you do this, you'll lose God. Peace, not violence, is the way,' I explained.

He looked at me for a moment, nodded and then walked off.

A teacher at the school told me that it wasn't unusual to have a lot of kids off school for six weeks at a time due to having been kneecapped, either with a bullet or a baseball bat. This was usually because they had either caused vandalism, nicked cars or bought drugs from someone who wasn't working for the paramilitaries.

We then went to see Father Gerry McCloskey at the Church of St Agnes on the Falls Road in Andersonstown, one of the most republican areas of Belfast. Just a few doors along from the church are the Sinn Fein offices. And daubed in paint on the wall of the Halifax building society opposite the church were the words 'English f*** off'. We wanted to talk to him about running a retreat in the parish later in the year.

The housekeeper introduced herself and said that she'd come in the car with us and give us a tour of the area, pointing out various places where bombs had gone off and people had been killed. As we drove around, she revealed that she'd witnessed four people being shot dead. Her granddaughter had seen one of the murders with her and was now having counselling because it had traumatised her so much. Spotting a statue of Our Lady on a roundabout on the Falls Road, I mentioned that this was unusual. She explained that a former IRA member had done this on all the roundabouts on the Falls Road after he experienced a conversion. Looking at the people walking along the streets, I felt that there was a great pain in Belfast, almost like oppression.

'I love Belfast,' said the housekeeper. 'I've lived here all my life. But if the peace process breaks down, I will leave the city.'

Padraig and I then drove to Omagh in County Tyrone, where, in 1999, a bomb had gone off in the town killing twenty-nine people. We were there to run a one-day retreat at Sacred Heart School. About 160 kids turned up, far more than I'd anticipated. Emmet, a local dentist, and the brother of Damien, who I'd lived with at St Joan of Arc in London, closed his practice for a few hours and joined us to provide some music. He'd also been a guitarist in a successful band at one time. He told me that the bomb had, in fact, brought the Catholics and Protestants closer together.

It had been arranged for me to appear as a guest on 'The Kelly Show' on Ulster TV. As this was the most popular chat show in Ireland, I was thrilled. It would enable me to tell a couple of million people about what Youth 2000 was doing.

When I arrived at the TV studios I was taken to the make-up room and then to the green room. I didn't feel nervous until I was making me way down a corridor to the studio when one of the production team called out to me, 'How does it feel to be about to speak to a couple of million people?'

Hearing my name called, I walked out into the bright lights of the studio to the sound of applause from the audience. I took my seat and then Gerry Kelly introduced me and asked me to say a bit about myself.

After I talked about my life and faith, he said to me, 'Well, we have our own gangsters here.' He was talking about the IRA and UVF.

204

'When I was a gangster I was only interested in money, power and greed,' I said, 'and I never hid behind a cause. But I think your gangsters are also only interested in money, power and greed, but they hide behind a cause and terrorise communities.'

I knew that the IRA and UVF were behind a lot of the drug trade in Northern Ireland. If you want drugs, then you have to buy them off paramilitary dealers. If you don't, then you're in trouble. It was exactly the same way as the drug trade used to operate in the pubs and clubs I'd worked at in London. If anyone tried to sell drugs without permission, we'd break them. If anyone tries to sell drugs without permission from the IRA or UVF, they'll get the same treatment. The IRA and UVF are simply a cover for organised crime. It's not about a cause or defending a country.

But in recent years, many paramilitaries have renounced violence and turned to God. One day in Belfast I met Mark Lenihan, a former member of the IRA who had carried out a number of punishment shootings and had served five years in prison. He told me that he'd turned his back on violence after visiting Medjugorje, where he'd experienced the power of God in his life. He's now a teacher and trying to persuade young kids not to get involved in violence.

I welcomed the opportunity to give a talk in Maghaberry, a modern, high-security prison in Lisburn, ten miles west of Belfast. I spoke about how violence could not bring peace in Northern Ireland.

Afterwards a stocky man came up to me and said in a reproachful voice, 'I didn't like what you said about the para-militaries.'

'It's Jesus Christ who speaks through me,' I replied. 'So if you've got a problem, take it up with him.'

He stared at me for a few moments and then said, 'Respect.'

As I was leaving the prison, the priest who had invited me in said, 'What did that man say to you after the talk?'

When I told him, he shook his head and said, 'Thank God for that. He's the head of the Continuity IRA.'

'He was?'

'Yes, and with one phone call he could have had you killed.'

'My eyes have been opened,' Padraig said, as we headed down the A1 from Belfast to Dublin.

'What do you mean?' I asked.

'Before coming to the north I had tended to see the IRA as sort of freedom fighters; a bit like the old IRA in the south who were fighting for their homeland. But I don't see them like that now. I had been believing in a myth.'

'Well, like you, I was given a lie as well. I had thought there was no discrimination against Catholics in Northern Ireland. The British media had always portrayed them as the problem. But I've now seen that when it comes to things such as housing and schools they aren't treated as well as the Protestants.'

During the following weeks, articles about me appeared in a number of newspapers and magazines, including the *Irish Independent*, *Sunday World* and *Bible Alive*. I also gave interviews to a lot of local radio stations and appeared on a live breakfast show on TV3 in Dublin. All of this helped to promote the work I was doing with Youth 2000. I was aware of the dangers of becoming a celebrity, so I always tried to talk about three things: the Eucharist, Our Lady and confession. If I managed this, then I viewed it as a success. If I only managed two of them, then it was two-thirds a success. It was the message of God's love that I wanted to get across, not how wonderful I was. Because I wasn't.

I was invited to appear on 'Life on the Rock', a youth programme of Eternal Word Television Network (EWTN), the world's largest Catholic broadcaster. I flew from Shannon Airport to Atlanta. A limousine met me and I was driven to the EWTN studio complex in Irondale, a few miles away, where I was given a room in the guest house.

Bill Bilton, a very chatty, down-to-earth guy in his late sixties, who was in charge of EWTN, explained to me that it was set up by Mother Angelica in 1981 in the garage of her monastery. It's grown amazingly since then. Today, it employs around three hundred staff, has an annual budget of $30 million and broadcasts in both English and Spanish to 66 million households in forty-three countries. It also broadcasts short wave radio programmes.

Father Andrew, who had been my spiritual director when I was with the Franciscan Friars of the Renewal, arrived the next day to record some programmes. It was great to see him again. That evening, we both went to have a drink with Father Mitch Patwa at his house on the complex. A very bright Jesuit who wears a ten-gallon Texas cowboy hat, he presents a number of biblical programmes on EWTN. I found him a fascinating man and was amazed to learn that he spoke Aramaic, the language of Jesus.

The author and speaker Scott Hahn was also staying in the guest house. I was very impressed by how approachable and real he was, considering he was so well known.

One morning, I drove to Hancecille, about half an hour from the studios, to meet Christina, a friend of Stacey's, who was now a member of the Poor Clares of Perpetual Adoration at the Monastery of Our Lady of the Angels, situated next to the shrine of the Most Blessed Sacrament.

Christina and I chatted through a grill, something that is still very common with Poor Clares. Several of the other sisters gathered around, laughing and joking. I was amazed at how young they were.

'You probably heard that Stacey and I aren't together any more,' I said when we were on our own.

'Yes,' she said.

'I think I hurt her.'

'She would have learned lots of lessons, John.'

'Do you think I should write to her and apologise for not giving her the time and care that I should have done?' I asked.

'I think you should pray about that.'

As I drove back to EWTN, I thought about the conversation

and whether I should write to Stacey. I felt that to do this might open up the wounds, so I decided not to, even though I was deeply sorry for the fact that I may have hurt her. I now knew that I wasn't able to open myself up to her because of my brokenness. I felt that, because of the hurt I'd experienced in my childhood, and even though I had experienced much healing, there was a fear in me of allowing someone to really love me.

Back in Ireland, I was interviewed on Talkback Radio in Belfast, and the subject of clerical sexual abuse came up.

'How dare you proclaim about Jesus Christ when all your priests are abusing kids,' challenged the presenter after I'd explained about my work as an evangelist.

'For a start, that's a vast exaggeration,' I replied firmly. 'In Ireland during the last ten years only eight priests have been convicted of abusing kids. So I don't know why you think all priests are guilty of abuse.'

'So you think they should all go free?'

'No. We have a judicial system. If a priest has broken the law, he should be punished. But he shouldn't be victimised and cast out as a leper. We live in a completely immoral society and we point the finger at anyone who is broken. To me, God's mercy is there for everyone.'

'What, even those monsters who abuse children?' he cut in.

'We should never make anyone out to be a monster. When I was a vicious gangster I don't know how many kids I hurt through the drugs and the other stuff I was involved in. But God's mercy is there, even for someone like me. And I know how much pain and guilt I had to go through because of the sins of my past.'

I remembered a story a priest friend in Wales told me about when Sister Briege McKenna came to his parish to give a talk. She asked him if he knew where she had just come from. No, he answered. She then told him she'd been to see a priest who had been sentenced to seven years in prison for abusing children. Then she added, 'None of you priests have been to see him in the two years he's been in prison, yet you call yourselves Christians. And do you know what he's doing every day? He's praying and saying Mass for those children he abused. He's repented of his sins.' The next day, the priest went to visit him. With any sin, no matter how terrible, I always think of Jesus' words: 'Let him who is without sin cast the first stone.'

It's easy to feel burnt out when you are on the road so much, so I was delighted when Emmet invited Padraig and I to join him and Declan for four days on his boat, which he was going to sail up the River Shannon from Carrick-on-Shannon to Lough Erne. It was brilliant. There was nothing to do except relax and admire some of Ireland's most beautiful scenery. At Devenish Island, which contains some ancient monastic ruins, including an Augustinian abbey and a twelfth-century round tower, we went ashore and prayed Morning Prayer. Looking around, I thought to myself that this might have been the first time the divine office had been said here in hundreds of years. The four of us talked honestly about our struggles in following Jesus. At night, we'd tie the boat up and have a barbecue and a bottle of wine sitting on the river bank, and Emmet would play his guitar.

I asked Padraig one night if he ever prayed to be healed.

'Yes, I pray to be healed every day, John, but I never pray to be healed of my spina bifida,' he replied.

'Why?'

'Because this is what makes me who I am.'

Feeling renewed, Padraig and I then travelled to Knock, in County Mayo, home to Ireland's major Marian shrine. We had one talk lined up at a local school, but nothing else planned afterwards. We found a convent and booked in for the night. It was very shabby though, so, because we liked our creature comforts, we moved to The Knock House, a lovely hotel near the shrine complex. The manageress told us we could have a room at a reduced rate because we were working for Youth 2000. But Padraig and I nearly had an argument that night because we were keeping each other awake with our snoring. We laughed about it over breakfast in the morning and decided to ask the manageress for separate rooms.

After the talk at the school, the chaplain told us that he would get us into lots of schools in the area. We stayed at Knock for a week and went into different schools each day. One afternoon, I gave a talk to twenty-six RE teachers at the St John's Pastoral Centre at the shrine. I encouraged them to give the kids the truth of the Catholic Church and not water it down. I told them that Father Benedict Groeschel once said to me that the greatest regret of his life and his priesthood was not being outrageous enough with the truth, and that Mother Teresa said that the more outrageous with the truth we are, the more outrageous God is with his miracles. Afterwards, a number of them asked if we would visit their schools.

We then drove to the west coast. After one-day retreats at schools in Tralee, the county town of Kerry, and on the beautiful Dingle Peninsula, with its mountains, early Christian oratories, and views out to the Blasket Islands, we then drove through Killarney, Mallow and Waterford across to Cortna-cuddy in County Wexford, on the other side of the country, to run a retreat in the parish of Father Jim Finn. Father Jim is a very prayerful and inspiring priest who allows the local youngsters to treat his presbytery as a second home.

About twenty-five kids turned up. We held all night ador-ation and I asked each kid to pledge an hour.

One of them said to me indignantly, 'All we've done is pray. We've never done so much praying in our life.'

'I make no apologies, because the more you pray the quicker you meet Jesus,' I answered.

On the Sunday, ten kids gave their testimony about how they had met Jesus. The others would have done as well if we'd had more time left.

Padraig and I prayed together a lot and tried to get to daily Mass while we were on the road. We also tried to do a holy hour when we could. We had a very similar outlook and we both loved our creature comforts, so there was none of this sleeping on the floor business. If we had a few days off we'd stay at his house in Dublin. I'd spend my time meeting with friends, mooching around the city centre or visiting Father Adrian Crowley.

I have to admit that I've always found it a struggle to use my spare time in a positive way. During this free time in Dublin, I had to be careful that I didn't give in to the temptation to surf around the TV channels and indulge in lustful thoughts or idle my time away gambling on the fruit machines in the amusement arcades.

There were occasions when I wondered if I'd made the right decision over Stacey. One night, I watched the film *Notting Hill*, a romantic comedy starring Hugh Grant and Julia Roberts. Did I make a mistake by ending the relationship? I asked myself. But then I thought of all the miracles I'd seen take place in people's lives, and I concluded that *Notting Hill* was sentimental hogwash.

Not everyone I came across liked the approach Padraig and I had to evangelisation. We went to do a two-day retreat at a school near Kilkenny. The first day went brilliantly. But that night a teacher phoned me. 'I think the retreat was too heavy,' she said.

'What do you mean?'

'We don't want you back tomorrow. But we'll give you a donation.'

'Well, what's too heavy? We had the kids for forty-five minutes in the morning and an hour in the afternoon.'

'Well, I don't think confession is appropriate,' she said.

After this incident, Padraig and I decided to make the retreats one day instead of two. This way, by the time any teachers objected to what we were doing, the retreat would be over.

Another time, in Navan, an RE teacher told me that he didn't believe in God.

'So what are you doing taking an RE post in a Catholic school if you don't believe in God?'

'Well, they didn't have a history post.'

'I think it's a disgrace. To me, you shouldn't be teaching about a faith you don't believe in.'

'Maybe this year I'll be converted,' he replied sarcastically.

I said to him, 'Well, one day you are going to have to stand before God. And you will have to explain why you haven't given the young people he has put in your care knowledge about the love of Jesus Christ.'

In March 2002, Padraig and I were joined by Breda, who had given up her job as a lab technician to come on the road with us, and Jason, the Youth 2000 regional leader in Belfast. Jason was brought up in a Protestant family in Portadown. When he became a Catholic, it caused a lot of friction .

At the end of our six months on the road, Padraig and I both felt that it had been a time of tremendous blessings and that we had both come to a deeper understanding of Christ. Despite his spina bifida, and the medication he had to take, he never once complained. He was a great witness.

'What have you learned from being on the road, brother?' I asked Padraig, as I drove through Phoenix Park in Dublin to the ferry terminal at North Wall.

'Well,' he began, 'and I know you won't take offence at this, but I've not met anyone so broken through whom God can work so many miracles.'

I laughed. 'You reckon?'

'Yes. I've spent the last three years of my life trying to be perfect rather than trying to be myself. I've realised by being with you, John, that true holiness comes from being yourself.'

'It's true, Padraig. God's not asking us to be plastic saints. He wants us to be who we really are. It took me ages to realise that.'

Arriving back in England, I spent a few days with my parents in London and then drove up to Norfolk for the New Dawn Conference in Walsingham. While I was there, I felt that God wanted me to set up a community in Ireland. Breda and several other young people had expressed interest in living in community.

So a few weeks later, myself, Breda, along with Patrick, Rory, Natalie, and Maura went to stay with the Little Sisters of the Poor at their convent in Sybil Hill Road, Dublin, until we found a house to live in. We'd only been there a few weeks when Sean Ascough, a businessman who was involved with Youth 2000, offered us the use of his modern four-bedroom house just outside Eniscorthy, a small town on the banks of the River Slaney in County Wexford, until it was sold.

I made Frank Duff, the founder of the Legion of Mary, the patron of the community. I chose him because I felt he had amazing faith and courage. He used to go to the brothels in the Dublin docks and literally fight to take the girls away to the hostel he'd established. Each of us made a commitment to live in community for a year. We started going out to schools in teams of three. I'd lead one team and Breda the other. We never charged for retreats. Instead we relied on donations.

I took all the ideas from the communities I'd lived in – the Franciscan Friars of the Renewal, the Family House of Prayer, St Austin's, Youth 2000 in England – and developed a programme for community living. We had holy hour in the morning, during which we recited Morning Prayer, and then we went to Mass in St Aidan's Cathedral. We'd pray the rosary together later in the day and then Evening Prayer and Night Prayer. We'd also pray the Divine Mercy prayer and have an open examination of conscience at the end of the day, where, sitting around the open fire in the living room, we would openly share our failings and thank God for our blessings.

We were all at different points in our faith journey. As in Liverpool, I was having to learn how to run the community without controlling people. One of the things I found difficult was that I had little support. I was not only in charge of the formation but I also had to make sure that we had enough money to eat and live. I found this stressful and sometimes took it out on the other community members.

One morning, as we were all about to leave for Mass in Eniscorthy, Maura said to me, 'Why are you smoking?'

'What do you mean?'

'There's only twenty minutes before Mass, and you're supposed to fast for an hour.'

'You take care of your own spiritual life and I'll take care of mine!' I snapped back and stormed out of the house to the car. During the short drive to the cathedral no one said anything. They could all see what a temper I was in. I could tell that Maura was upset by my outburst.

After Mass, I prayed in front of the statue of Our Lady of Lourdes. 'You have to sort out my community. It's in a mess.' I felt her say, 'It's not your community. It's mine.' I knew that I had to let go. I was too hard on the other members. From that point on, I resolved to say to God in prayer, 'Sort out your community.'

In any community you will get personality clashes and ours was no different. I began to realise that some of the members needed a more loving environment to help them grow rather than to be in a very high-pressured community with a hectic schedule of retreats each day where we were living out of each other's pockets.

To build up the community, we went to Mount Melleray, a Cistercian monastery in County Waterford, for a silent retreat. The monks here live a traditional monastic life which is centred on prayer. But I've come across some religious orders using yoga and reiki. I remember a priest I know being asked what he thought about these sorts of things. He said, 'You have the Eucharist, confession, Our Lady, the teachings of the Church, you've got the wonders of the sacraments, adoration and it's still not enough. Put your effort into this before looking at this rubbish.'

After giving a talk one morning in a school in County Clare,

I noticed that a seventeen-year-old lad seemed to be in a lot of turmoil. It was written all over his face. I asked him what his name was. When he told me, I said I'd pray for him.

Later on, a teacher came up to me and said the lad wanted to talk to me. I went into a classroom on my own with him. We sat down and I offered him a ciggy. He then opened up to me. He told me that his dad was an alcoholic who often beat him up and also his mum and younger brother.

'You spoke about this loving God. But where is he in all this pain?' he said angrily.

'He's you. He's suffering because you're suffering. He doesn't want anyone to hurt us. He wants us to love each other. But he won't take away our freedom to choose. And he won't take away the freedom of your dad to drink and then take it out on you and your mum and brother.'

'So what can I do?'

'You can get help. There are counsellors out there. I can help you to find someone.'

He put his head in his hands. 'I've had enough. I can't take it anymore. My life's a mess. I'm taking dope and downers. I feel depressed and even suicidal sometimes.'

Seeing the anguish on his face, I thought of the crucified Christ and said, 'Jesus is being crucified because you're being crucified. Know that he loves you.'

After chatting with him for a while longer, I then said that I'd arrange for him to meet a priest I knew who would be able to help him.

One of my favourite places in Ireland is the city of Derry, which stands on the River Foyle. Its high fortified walls date from the seventeenth century when Catholic forces of King James II blockaded the Protestant supporters of William of Orange for fifteen weeks, leading to thousands of deaths. I think St Columba's Church, Long Tower, is one of the most beautiful in Ireland, and it was on this site that St Columba said his first Mass in the sixth century. But, like many places in Northern Ireland, it has been scarred by the troubles. In

1972 British troops entered the Bogside, a Catholic housing estate, and shot dead thirteen demonstrators and wounding a further seventeen. This became known as 'Bloody Sunday'.

Yet while I was in the city, I saw signs of hope for peace in the north. One night, I attended a rosary group at the Carmelite St Joseph's Retreat House in Termonbacca. For the last seventeen years, people have been meeting here each week to say the rosary for peace. It was the idea of Patrick Hume, the brother of David Hume, the leader of the Socialist Democratic Labour Party who, along with David Trimble, the leader of the Ulster Unionist Party, instigated the peace process. When I was asked to give a talk, I said to the group that they, and all the other prayer groups, both Catholic and Protestant, were the real peace process.

While at a healing service in Buncrana, a small resort on the beautiful Inishowen Peninsula amidst the mountains of northern Donegal, I looked around at all the broken people sitting there and the picture of Christ that I'd seen in the Regina Caeli hostel in Dublin flashed before my eyes. It was as if Our Lady was saying to me that I was doing what Christ was doing in that picture: bringing all her broken children to her son in the Blessed Sacrament.

I was now receiving numerous requests to give talks in various churches around Ireland. This meant that I'd travel on my own and often stay overnight somewhere. I realised that this could be an excuse to run away from the community. So I decided to take one of the community with me if I had to give a talk. This is what the Franciscan Friars of the Renewal do when they travel, so that they can support each other.

I've always been passionately committed to pro-life work, so I was pleased when Patrick McCrystal, director of Human Life International, asked if the community would visit eleven towns and cities around Ireland and speak about the right to life from the moment of conception to natural death. In other words, abortion, contraception and euthanasia. The talks were held in hotels and hundreds of people turned up each night.

Just before Christmas 2002, Neil phoned to say that he had decided to leave the Community of the Beatitudes. 'It's been a great grace, John, but I feel I need to move on.'

'Why don't you join the community here,' I suggested. I knew that Neil would fit in and that his faith and spiritual maturity would benefit the other members.

'You mean it?'

'Yeah. It would be great to have you here.'

I said to Paul Rooney that we needed to produce a pamphlet for schools and parishes explaining what we did as a mission team. He liked the idea, but wondered how we were going to afford it. After Mass on New Year's Eve at St Aidan's Cathedral, I was at the Family of Adoration convent in Ferns when a man called John Roche came up to me and said that he had listened to one of my tapes.

'It was very inspiring,' he said.

'Thanks,' I replied.

'If ever I can help you, give me a shout,' he said, handing me his business card.

Looking at it, and seeing that he was a printer, I thought he was touting for business. 'Well, we haven't got much money.'

'No. If you need any printing done, I'll do it for nothing.'

We met for lunch the next day at a hotel alongside the river in Eniscorthy and I described to him what I wanted printing.

'That's no problem John. Let me have a draft of what you want produced.'

John Roche believes in applying high ethical principles to his company. He told me that when he met his accountant one day he was informed that his profits were going down. He asked what percentage of his business profits had been given away the previous year. Fifteen per cent, replied the accountant. Well, said John, we need to give away twenty per cent this year. His accountant looked puzzled. 'It's because we haven't given enough away that the profits are down,' said

John. On another occasion, he landed a job worth a quarter of a million euros, about a hundred and seventy thousand quid. But when he looked more closely at the leaflets he had been asked to print, he saw that they were supporting abortion. So he phoned up the sales rep and told him that he wouldn't take the job, as it would be promoting something that was evil.

A couple of weeks later, we received several hundred attractive pamphlets from John. Once again, God had provided.

Neil joined after Christmas. At first, some of the community members didn't seem sure about him, but they soon warmed to him and he became a great support not just for me but for everyone else.

In April, Maura left the community to help look after her dad, who had cancer, and Lily from Carlow joined. Rory and Natalie then left in June, both of them feeling that they had grown a lot during their time in community. Caroline, who had quit her job in Galway, then joined us.

When Mel Gibson's film *The Passion of the Christ* came out I was invited to attend a special viewing at a cinema in Lucan, a suburb of Dublin. As I sat there, I found it hard to watch because I could see how my sins had affected Christ. One of the most moving parts for me was the scene when Mary ran to Jesus. It showed her love for him and how much Mary loves each one of us.

After several months of giving talks in schools during the week and running retreats or parish missions at the weekend, I was feeling exhausted and, as we'd had a few tensions in the community, a bit fed up. I was wondering what the point of it all was. Kneeling before Jesus in a church in Derry one evening during a reconciliation service, I prayed, 'Does what we do make a difference? Is there a point to it?'

Just then I felt a tap on my shoulder. Looking round, I saw an elderly man standing there. 'There's a woman in the sacristy who wants to speak to you.'

So I left the pew and made my way into the sacristy, where a smartly dressed woman was waiting.

'Hello,' I greeted her, wondering what she wanted.

'Is your name John Pridmore?'

'Yeah,' I nodded.

'Were you in a school in Claudy today?'

'Yeah, I was.'

'Well, my fifteen-year-old daughter tried to slash her wrists two weeks ago. She went back to school today and she wore a jumper to hide the stitches. She told me over forty-five minutes every single word you said in that school. At the end of it you said you can choose life in Jesus Christ or you can choose death, which is living without him.'

'That's right,' I said.

She then began to cry. 'She said to me, "Mum I chose life. I'm going to go back to Mass, pray the rosary with you and go to your prayer group." I saw my daughter die when she was twelve because she stopped praying and believing in God. And I saw her alive again today. You don't know how valuable what you are doing in schools is. Never stop it.'

Going back into the reconciliation service, I felt very emotional and that God had answered my prayer. I then thought of something Mother Teresa had said when a journalist asked why she did what she did with the poor and dying in Calcutta. He said that what she did was only like a drip in a bucket. Mother Teresa replied that if everyone did the little bit that God asked them to do then the bucket would be overflowing and the world would be healed through love.

Epilogue

THIS IS AN UPDATE on the final chapter, which charted my life up to 2003. While writing this epilogue, I've been thinking that I must have spoken to well over a million people on my travels – quite a daunting but amazing thought! These last five years have truly been an incredible time on my journey of faith.

Probably the most significant development for me has been setting up St Patrick's Community in Ireland, where I now live. The community really grew out of the Youth 2000 mission team. I found a group of young people who, like me, wanted to live a life centred on the eucharist and prayer and take the message of Jesus to parishes and schools.

The first thing we had to do was to find a property. We didn't have a clue where we would end up living. Thanks to God's providence, and the generosity of Bishop Colm O'Reilly, we were given a former presbytery set in beautiful rolling countryside in County Leitrim. It even had a small church next door. It was just what we wanted.

When we first moved into the house, some of the locals were a bit suspicious of us. Rumours soon circulated that a bunch of hippies had arrived. I found this amusing and responded by putting the word out that anyone was welcome to come for a cup of tea. It wasn't long before people started popping in. Now, we're very much part of the local community. Mind you, we're not there much of the time. Most weeks, we're on the road running missions in parishes and schools.

There are currently five of us living in the community. Apart from me, there's Neil, who has been a good friend of mine since we first met in London's East End many years ago; Breda, who comes from County Tipperary and is a gifted singer and musician; Matthew, from Milwaukee in the US, who had a powerful experience of God after finding that endless partying had left him feeling empty; and Catherine, whose faith really came alive when she began attending prayer meetings at university.

And there have been some very blessed moments for us during the missions we've run. In 2005 when we did a five-day mission at Mullingar cathedral, the sacristan turned to me and said that he'd never seen so many people there. It was packed every night. On the Tuesday evening 25 priests were on hand to hear confessions.

When we went to do a mission in Tuam in 2006, we invited all the kids at a local school to come to the cathedral later that evening. At the end of the reconciliation service, a 15 year old girl came up to me. She had tears in her eyes. In front of about a thousand people, she said, 'I thought I'd come to see what it was all about. I went to confession for the first time in ages. When I came out, I knew that God was real and that he loved me.'

Another time, I agreed to give a talk at a school in Dublin. A teacher there had been pestering me for about a year to visit. In the end, like the unjust judge in the gospel, I gave in to her. Around 600 kids turned up to hear me.

After I'd finished speaking, the teacher asked me, 'Why do you think I kept nagging you to come here?'

'I don't know,' I replied.

'A year ago, you came to the school where my son goes. He hadn't been to Mass since he was fourteen. He's now seventeen and he goes not just on Sundays but also in the week,' she said. 'I wanted you to be able to have the same effect on the kids here as you did on him,' she said.

I felt touched and humbled. It's moments like this, and the

one with the girl who came up to me in the cathedral in Mullingar, that really give me hope when I'm feeling tired by all the travelling up and down Ireland, or when I'm feeling that God can't use me.

Our community has also travelled outside of Ireland. I led a youth retreat in the Netherlands and also gave a number of talks at World Youth Day in Cologne in 2005, where I got my first glimpse of Pope Benedict XVI. As well as this, I was invited to speak at conferences in Iowa and Cincinnati in the US. At a youth festival in Medjugorje, I spoke to my biggest crowd ever, around 30,000, and I received a standing ovation. As I stepped off the podium, Neil put his hand on my shoulder and said with a grin, 'Remember, Jesus used a donkey more than once.' He was reminding me not to let the applause go to my head. When Jesus rode into Jerusalem on a donkey, the donkey thought all the cheering was for him.

I also made my second visit to the Catholic TV station EWTN in Birmingham, Alabama, where I appeared on Life on the Rock and Journey Home. As a result of the programmes, I received invitations to give talks elsewhere in the US and also in New Zealand and Switzerland.

Something else unexpected happened. A Hollywood film producer contacted me. He said that he'd read From Gangland to Promised Land and wanted to raise the money needed to turn it into a movie. He's since been working hard to do this, and has found a famous actor who would be interested in playing me. I have to admit that it's a strange feeling to know that you might be portrayed on the big screen. But as far as I'm concerned, it's all in God's hands.

Someone who continues to provide great support for my work is John Roche, who runs a printing company. Thanks to him and Xt3, I now have 5,000 copies of From Gangland to Promised Land to give to anyone who can't afford to pay for a copy and also to inmates when I visit prisons.

Having served time behind bars, I know how important it is to be given hope and to be told that you matter to God. I've seen God touch many of the hardest prisoners during the talks I've given. This just underlines that it's often when someone reaches rock bottom that they're most open to God. A chaplain at a young offenders' prison in Lancashire told me about a young guy who was serving a sentence for vicious attack on his father. After reading From Gangland to Promised Land, he underwent a profound experience of God and, when he was released from prison, was reconciled with his father.

Since 2005 St Patrick's Community has been involved with Mary's Meals (www.marysmeals.org), a fantastic charity that provides around 300,000 meals a day to children in Africa, Asia, Eastern Europe and Latin America. It was founded by my friend Magnus McFarlane-Barrow, who's an amazing guy. In October 2007, we visited Limerick, Cork, Derry, Belfast and Drumcondra to talk about the real difference the money it raises is making to some of the poorest children in the world. I wasn't sure how many people would turn up at the venues we'd booked, but each night was blessed. Our community has now raised 370,000 euros for Mary's Meals.

The following month, my second book was published, A Gangster's Guide to God. I was over the moon when Cardinal Cormac Murphy-O'Connor agreed to attend the launch at Westminster Cathedral Hall. He's someone I greatly admire and he's given me great encouragement in my work each time we've met. And the personal letter of endorsement he has given me has opened many doors to schools and parishes. I've also had some incredible feedback about the book, including from a priest who said that he was about to quit the priesthood. 'But when I read the book, I then realised that I needed to learn how to forgive.'

The publication of the book rounded off a very busy year, but one that produced many graces, both in my own life and in the lives of many of those who I met. To renew myself spiritually, I decided to spend Christmas with the Franciscan Friars of the Renewal in the South Bronx. The year I spent there was probably one of the most important in my life, and each time I've since been back to visit the friars I've drawn great strength from seeing how they live out their lives in such a radical way for Jesus. I was lucky to be able to spend some time with Father Benedict Groeschel and Father Bernard Murphy, two men of great wisdom and spiritual insights. They both reminded me that no matter how busy I might be, or how many things I have on my to do list, I must make time each day for prayer. For if we don't pray, we lose our relationship with God.

And prayer will be one of the themes that I'll be talking about when I travel to Sydney in 2008 to take part in World Youth Day. I'm looking forward to my first trip to Australia – I was looking forward to surfing until Neil told me it would be winter!

If you're interested in finding out more about what I'm up to, then visit:

- *www.xt3.com* – come and join me and many others on this fantastic social networking platform for World Youth Day Sydney and beyond; or

- *www.johnpridmore.com* – my personal website for info and more; and

For information about St Patrick's Community, go to *www.stpatrickscommunity.org*

God bless

John Pridmore
April 2008

Quotes and Testimonies

Extracts from emails sent to John:

"Hi John, You came to our school this morning… and talked to us about your life. We just wanted to thankyou for the talk you gave it was very eye opening. We have great respect for you because you had the strength to admit you had done bad things in your life but you tried to make it right and succeeded. It made us grateful for what we have and gave us faith in God…"

– from two students at secondary school in UK

"… I also used to work the door at various bars when I was younger. I can relate to some of that lifestyle although yours was a little crazier than mine… I am a halfway through your book. It is a phenomenal read …"

– from a police officer on Long Island

"Hello John, You visited my school one day last week. The talk you did was absolutly amazing!
I enjoyed practically every aspect of the talk, at the end you told me to keep smiling and i havn't stopped since! You looked rather scary at first but inside you reminded me a bit of my dad. I have read nearly all of your book and i can't seem to put it down! …"

– from a teenager in UK

"… Last November my daughter married a man who had met you in London when you were a bad boy shall we say. He was on the fringes of that life too. He told me he met you after your conversion and could not believe the change in you… He is in the process of putting his life back together. He is reading your first book and getting great encouragement especially when he is inclined to give in to bad habits…"

– from a mother in Ireland

"… I went to the Mission at St. Simon's last night and you signed one of your books for me.
I am so glad that I went to it. It actually moved me to tears, I was overwhelmed by something I can't describe. I felt like I had been waiting my whole life (well 15 years) to go to that church. I felt like I really belonged there… I feel like a changed person, like I've finally properly found God…"

– from the UK

Reviews of 'From Gangland to Promised Land' on Amazon:

"I read in the TES about John Pridmore and how he left behind a life of crime so I decided to give his book a go. And it was a knockout read. This guy really lived the gangster lifestyle. I squeamed at some to the descriptions of the fights he was in. He was very brutal. But today he is a changed man, advocating peace and prayer. As an English teacher, I was impressed by how well Greg Watts told his story. The narrative fairly raced along. I think the book may become a classic of its kind."

"This is one of the best books I've read for ages. It's a real page-turner. I've read books by Dave Courtney, Vic Dark and other hard men, but this is a gangster story with some real depth to it."

EPILOGUE

"I had tears in my eyes when I finished reading From Gangland to Promised Land. I then read it again the next day. It's an extraordinary story and one that would make a great film. It has everything: edge of your seat stuff, deeply moving moments, struggles and inspiration. A brilliant book!"

"A friend in Ireland sent me this book, as I like crime stories. But while this is a crime story, It's not like any I've read before. It's fantastic and inspiring! I've now lent it to a mate at work."

"Wow! This is a brilliant book. I only picked it up by chance when I walked into a local bookshop. I read a couple of pages and liked the style… At times, the story is quite brutal, but it's well handled by author Greg Watts."

If you enjoyed From Gangland to Promised Land you might like to read Gangster's Guide to God, available through Amazon

GANGSTER'S GUIDE TO GOD

John Pridmore with Greg Watts

Join

Connect with Millions.
Share the Experience.
Build a Better World.

Live World Youth Day Every Day.